Foreword by John Edward

Finding My Ruby Slippers

A Soul's Journey to Self-Love

MaryAnna Nardone

The Three Tomatoes Book Publishing

Published February 2024
ISBN: 979-8-9891962-7-2
Library of Congress Control Number: 2024903589

For information address:
The Three Tomatoes Book Publishing
6 Soundview Rd.
Glen Cove, NY 11542

Cover design: Susan Herbst
Cover photo: iStock

Dedication

In memory of my brother Mark.
And for my sons, Vincent and Mark.

Table of Contents

Foreword

When I was asked by MaryAnna to read her book, I was excited because we have been friends for so long that she is family. I sat down to read it on a flight back from a recent tour of Australia and within a few chapters I found myself tearing up on more than one occasion. When you know a person, know their story, and know their work it is hard to elicit that type of visceral reaction. Not only did I have this burst of emotion and discovery of new things about MaryAnna, but I had to immediately log on to the plane's Wi-Fi to communicate with her about it.

I bombarded her with a series of reactions and questions. I had to tell my sister-in-spirit that I was so impressed with her vulnerability and intention to teach. I found my tears turned to laughter and then surprise when she released an arsenal of her expertise that I wasn't even aware of. It sure explained why I would feel such amazing energy when she worked on me.

The role of any metaphysical practitioner is to empower people with their knowledge, practice, and procedures. My motto with my work as a psychic medium is always to leave people better than I found them, to empower through reading, teaching, and sharing my personal experiences; this book does just that.

With MaryAnna (surrogate Dorothy) as our guide, in search of her own ruby slippers we follow her very complex yellow brick road far beyond Emerald City in search of the ultimate achievement...self-love.

Along our journey we see how MaryAnna encounters her own Tin Man, Cowardly Lion, and Scarecrow while she battles the flying monkeys we all encounter in life. The result is the reader is all of them as she finds the heart, courage, strength, and intellectual fortitude to discover the greatest accomplishment we are all seeking while here in the physical form...enlightenment.

There are emotional moments of reflection MaryAnna allows us to have about our own life's journey as she reflects and shares the pain of loss and long-term effects of grief through death and divorce, while persevering and building a life on a spiritual foundation.

As many books will pontificate on how if you follow these eight easy steps you will find health, wealth, etc., MaryAnna doesn't make promises—instead she provides insights, guidance, wisdom, and practical applications over a five-decade career.

If you are looking for a true body, mind, and soul handbook to feel beautiful on the inside and out, then finding your ruby slippers will show you your version of the home you can reside in.

~John Edward, psychic medium, author

Introduction

Mirror, Mirror on the Wall

A s we look into the mirror, it requires our vision—more importantly our eyes. What is that saying? Our eyes are the window to our soul. I will add to that by stating if the eyes are the window to our soul, then our eyelashes are the fluttering of our heart. What we see and how we view ourselves completely defines and creates who we are. Over the past thirteen years, I kept many journals. As I began to open them up slowly, I realized I didn't want to see some things I had written. I am amazed that those moments of journaling were actually my higher self talking.

It was a Tuesday, November 8, 2022, and I was in bed with the flu. All I kept thinking was *I wish I could go to the beach.* On that day I opened one that said November 8, 2018. I called this day my magical alignment. This is what I wrote in my journal that day.

"My solar return, such peaceful moments, my soul is in bliss—opening gifts of gratitude—God's plan. No more struggles as the mind has connected to my soul, serenity, passion, purpose. Healing hands inspiration, nonjudgment

Oakland Beach. *Know your greatness, congratulate your ability to release now anything that doesn't serve you with love.*

I was divinely led to this area by my thoughts of the beach and water, a place that always since childhood comforted me. For many years I ignored my soul's desires. Never really knowing why until I returned. Only then would I realize the aha moment of how much I missed being here. Summer of 2018, how did I become so disconnected from myself? This peaceful feeling, unlike any other one I have ever known, returned. And today November 8, 2018—it's my birthday. Once again, like many days I come and sit and meditate watching the beauty of nature. There is a stillness today on the water that is breathtaking, glass-like. I will now send out my intentions for this solar year... beginning now...

Perfect health for myself and my children and partners, financial freedom, everyday alignment with source. Dharma, my life purpose being blessed in every moment of this present existence for the gifts God has given me. I will make intentions every day to be on a path of love in all my actions and thoughts, amen."

Finding this journal was the best birthday gift I could ever get, that year of 2022. My angels and guides heard me... they led me to find this journal entry, and more importantly the message and promise I made to myself. Life can confuse us at times, and sometimes we can forget who we really are when we look into the mirror. I got a reality check that day... amen.

It was the beginning of me finding my ruby slippers, knowing just what was being reflected to me in my mirror—know thyself. It is a freedom that I will never take for granted. It was understanding my journey that I will be taking you through—my traumas, my guidance, the lessons, the adventures, the Earth angels I was gifted with on the way. It was recognizing that my passion and purpose is to help heal others, especially the Divine Feminine, which is the expansion of my own self-healing and finding my inner beauty.

I am honored to be writing this book that started back in 2010. You will notice I reference my friend John Edward often and his beautiful wife Sandra. They have been my guides for many years—John has been a brotherly influence and Sandra is like a sister to me. I have been blessed with their unconditional love and guidance for over twenty years. It is an interesting story of how we met.

In 1995, my sister and I had readings scheduled with John. My sister went first, and when she finished, I went into the reading room. John Edward looked at me and said, "I have to tell you your reading is most likely going to be the same as your sister. I really would like to reschedule it, as I don't feel comfortable taking a fee from you for basically the same reading."

I was devastated and replied, "Oh no, it must mean you have something bad to tell me." He reassured me, nothing bad at all was happening, and that he would get me back within a month or so. Although I was very disappointed, I realized what an amazing person he was to do that. Anyone else would have just continued to do the reading.

The next day at work, I was outside smoking a cigarette (a bad habit I had picked up during my divorce) with some of the dancers from a dance studio next to the spa where I was working. I began to tell them my story about John Edward from the night before and how authentic he was for not taking my fee. In addition to the dancers, there was another woman who I noticed for a moment, who was politely listening. After I finished the story, she introduced herself as John's wife, Sandra.

I thought I was going to pass out...WTF? Was I actually having this conversation with the wife of John Edward? I was in complete awe of her. She was this beautiful young woman, who by the way was not a smoker, and we clicked instantly and have been friends ever since. More importantly, she thanked me for my kind words about her husband, John. This was a huge synchronicity. It gave me goose bumps... nothing is a coincidence.

As a licensed medical aesthetician, I have studied skincare, treating different conditions, doing facials, and applying advanced skincare therapies, such as laser hair removal and chemical peels, to enhance the appearance of the skin. I had the privilege of owning my own boutique spa for twenty years. Along my journey to finding my ruby slippers, I've worked with celebrities and had many surreal moments like being on The Studios at Paramount set where makeup artists were using my skincare products on the actors and being at the Emmys gifting suite. I came to realize that celebrities are just people, and they, too, are finding their way beyond what may seem like a perfect lifestyle. I remember a day doing a treatment at my New York City location, trying to give comfort to a fabulous celebrity while she was on the phone for the entire time...and then pausing to ask me if I did the extraction and mask part. The degree of difficulty, as you may imagine, was hilarious yet stressful, as she was having a challenging day in her life.

I hope you will laugh and cry as you read my story and that it will invoke a spark, igniting a memory waking up your soul. We all have a divine birthright, which includes abundance, a vortex with everything we ever wanted. Finding it for some comes naturally, but for most of us it requires going into what I like to call "into the dermis, skin deep," (a metaphor for going within to discover the answers). Over the years of using my hands to treat the topical layer of the skin known as the epidermis, I discovered that my hands are one of my gifts of healing energy.

Finding purpose and passion—your true authentic beauty that we all possess—is powerful, potent, and completely divine, as you will discover. It doesn't come in a bottle—having a hands-on treatment with me can't give it to you. As you embark on this journey with me, I will teach you what I did to regain my passion, heal, forgive myself and others, and how I found my way back to my "Emerald City" (my *moving meditation*).

My intention is to give you the tools that worked for me. Imagine losing your love of singing, suddenly having no will to perform. A dancer who can't seem to find their rhythm, while filming *Dancing with the Stars* (a favorite of mine). A mom who can't get out of bed to get her kids ready for their day, the single mother who has no choice but to work three jobs. The schoolteacher who is standing in front of her class, dealing with the loss of a loved one, without any desire to teach. The hair salon owner who just got divorced, out drinking the night before trying a new hairstyle or color formula on you! We are every woman, regardless of our professions. We have all been through challenging life struggles. How do we find our way back? Every day, women battle breast cancer or ovarian cancer and they still have families to care for and jobs to continue. How do we recover from our life challenges?

My journey will show you how I lost my *moving meditation*. How do you learn? Heal? Forgive yourself? Money doesn't heal you. The wealthiest people are also just people who put their pants on one leg at a time and also deal with life challenges. Healing your traumas is vital for your expansion. Be consciously aware that you need to heal in order to not attract the same experience in a different form. When we don't address these issues more trauma and disease can occur as the body and mind are all related to creating your future.

This book is a teaching tool. My intention is that reading it will create space for you, it's just *you and me in my treatment room*. Let me be your guide...and like going to Vegas, "what happens there stays there." I used to tell that to my clients as I wanted them to know that the treatment room was *a sacred space, I was holding for them* to relax, release, and share without judgment.

Let me teach you what I now know...what took me to a new place that would be a sacred place of peace. Maya Angelou said, "When you know better, you do better." What's the point of going through all the pain, healing, and learning if not to share with others, guide them in a way that creates a ripple effect with the collective consciousness, for when we love ourselves fully, it enhances every soul, vibrating humanity to higher dimensions of love and light.

Buckle up y'all! As I invite you to come along with me on my journey to the Emerald City to find my ruby slippers.

> With love and blessings,
> MaryAnna

CHAPTER 1

Skin Deep

(Root Chakra)

L et's begin my journey. My dad passed away on November 2, 1991, just before my thirty-first birthday. It was a chaotic time, and it also woke me up from the illusion of being happily married. It's so interesting how the mind can compartmentalize issues of pain. Delusional most definitely. Looking back now, many years later, I now understand this was learned behavior.

I am a middle child with three siblings. I learned as a young child to be the fixer of things that were unsettling in my home. Somehow, I was the one to make difficult situations better—that was my role. My parents were very happy, however unhealed from their own childhood wounds. The biggest life trauma was when my oldest brother Mark passed away in 1984, at the age of twenty-six. I was twenty-three at the time, married with an eighteen-month-old. I still don't have words to explain the trauma we endured as a family.

Completely blindsided, we didn't see it coming. It was a rare lung disease that started with a cough—two weeks later he was gasping for air and died. It had started a few weeks earlier when he experienced pain in his shoulder and was admitted to the hospital. One evening, the whole family— my parents, sister, younger brother, and me—were at my brother's bedside. We were all chatting and for some reason I looked over at everyone, and I heard, *"This will be the last time you will all be together."* My immediate internal reaction was, *OMG, what a terrible thought*, and I immediately shut it down but deep in the dermis (my metaphor for deep inside) I felt a gut pain. I ignored it as best I could.

My brother had some tests that were all negative and ruled out cancer, which in those days somehow signaled all will be well. He was sent home. A wave of relief came over me. *Whew*, I thought, *OK, all will be OK*, thinking not having cancer meant he was out of the woods—until the morning of October 3, 1984.

I was the one to get the call from my brother. His last words, not really words, was him gasping for air. Both lungs had collapsed. I grabbed my eighteen-month-old son, buckled him into the car seat, and got there as fast as I could. Although it was less than one mile from my house, the trip felt like two years. When I arrived, he was at the front door and the moment he saw me running up the porch he collapsed. His face was blue. I called the ambulance, but no one was coming; I was all alone with him and my little boy. They finally arrived and put him in the ambulance. Now I had to get the family to the hospital.

I somehow got this surge of energy (adrenaline) and I was calm, most likely out of my body, and became a very logical person. My mom was out with her cousin, and I had no way of getting her—remember there were no cell phones in 1984. So I started by calling my dad first at his job where he was a teacher. I remember telling them at the front office to be sure to let him know it wasn't an emergency. My concern was for all to arrive safely, definitely my higher self was in charge. I was calm and frighteningly composed. I dropped my little boy off with Joann, my best friend of twenty-five years. Then, I don't know why, but I was directed to go through my mom's cousin's neighborhood where I could not find my mother.

After what seemed to be hours, I had to stop looking and drive to the hospital where my dad and younger brother had arrived. A priest was talking about life, and it was at that moment that I came back into my body. I began to say, "I need to see him, now." They tried to stop me, including my father. I could not express at that moment what I had seen about finding him. I ran down the hospital hall and found him. He looked like he was sleeping, except his sweatshirt was ripped where he was intubated. He was ice-cold—not as blue as I had seen him earlier.

My soul somehow left my body when I first entered the house and found him. I felt like I lost track of time—calling my dad at work, dropping my baby off, searching for my mother. Finally, I realized I had to get to the hospital to hear what my soul knew the moment I received his call, hearing a gasp or his last words. Then there was the realization that we had to tell my mom. My dad got very calm and guided my brother Andrew and me out to his car. We left our other vehicles at the hospital. My dad drove the three miles to his house and talked the whole time about my mom. It felt like an eternity getting there.

As we pulled into the driveway my mother was outside on the porch. I was confused by why she was already scream-ing, and then my dad said he called her cousin Shirley (I had told him Mom was with her). He told Shirley, "Mark died. Please prepare her," as he knew Shirley had lost her son five years earlier. Dad somehow knew it was not a coincidence my mom was having lunch with Shirley; she wasn't meant to find my brother or be at the hospital. It was a moment in time forever embedded in my soul, my mom wailing for what seemed to be hours, and then my dad said, "Someone has to go to the train station and pick up your sister." What began at 10:00 a.m. on that beautiful fall day, October 3, it was now already 6:30 p.m. My dad's ritual was to pick up my sister daily.

I definitely left my body at this point. It took me years to remember witnessing and recapitulating that drive home, my mom screaming over and over. I vaguely also remem-ber seeing my brother's flip-flops at the back door, think-ing, *This just can't be happening…he will never wear those again*. I also remember the hospital giving my dad his watch and wallet, thinking for a split second, *Why?* Then realizing, *Oh my God, it's those little things that were so profound*. My sister arrived back from the train and to this day, I still cannot recall that evening. My next memory was seeing him at the funeral parlor, while holding my parents up as we walked in as a family.

Almost thirty years later I would understand about severe trauma and soul fragmentation. I carried the guilt of not getting there fast enough, thinking I could have saved him. Repeating the events of that day and reliving it, over and over, still sends chills down my spine. My role was somehow to take care of everyone else. I know now that I went on autopilot. I wasn't in my body because if I had stopped for a minute I would have wanted to die. The only salvation was the essence of my young eighteen-month-old who kept me from going insane. I knew I had to fight the pain and help the family recover. My parents had just buried their firstborn. I guess somewhere, deep in my subconscious, I was a superhero.

I sometimes now I think, *How the hell did I do that?* Using my superpowers every day, the family went back to work, while I spent my days with my grieving mother and young son. My heart just didn't know how to help her. Never ever for a moment did I think of myself or my grief or the fact that I found him and the trauma I went through. *I lost my brother.* I would never ever be the same. You see, that was the time that I decided to shut my heart down. I didn't know I was actually doing that; however, it was the only way I knew to keep from falling down.

I just kept my focus on my beautiful son who kept me moving forward and made me laugh again. I cherished him every second of every day. Somewhere in that time I knew the joy my firstborn brought all of us, and I thought, *Imag-*

ine if I had another little human to love and bring joy back to the family? In January 1986, I gave birth to my second child. I named him Mark in honor of my brother. I knew this new little soul would be the best gift ever—he was, and both my sons are my gifts sent here in divine timing for me.

*****

Seven years later, on October 27, 1991, my sister got married. It was a red-carpet lifetime event for me. My sister and the whole family would be celebrating, and my boys were in the wedding. It was magical. My sister looked like Princess Diana, only she was Princess Irma. I remember so vividly dancing all night. At one moment, I caught my dad's gaze watching all of us with such joy I actually heard him say, "I am capturing this moment of love, for this is the last time we will all be together." The death of my brother Mark in 1984 was so devastating but the pain and sadness made our bond stronger than ever. We realized in the blink of an eye how saying I love you to each other every day was vital. If only once again, I had listened to my intuition. I heard my dad clear as day. I was again being prepared for what was to come next.

My intuition as a child and young adult was always on fire. The day before my dad passed, I had a terrible feeling something was wrong. After getting home from visiting him at the hospital, all I wanted to do was go back to the hospital. My dad needed a minor procedure that was scheduled for when my sister would be on her honeymoon. He made my mom and me promise not to tell my sister, so that her honeymoon would be wonderful. He did not want to take away from her happiness. I went against my intuition after visiting my dad—I knew something was wrong. When I returned home, I tried to tell my husband what I was feeling and that I wanted to go back to the hospital. My husband would not allow me to go back...just writing those words—*not allowed*—shows how I betrayed my soul in that moment, and many more times as you will read.

The next morning, the call came from the hospital to come immediately. I knew he was gone. My husband couldn't understand how I knew. For me, this was the beginning of the end, my heart hurt. He caused such anxiety the night before and I gave in because I saw my boys getting upset. Now I somehow had the job of getting my sister home from her honeymoon.

Chills came over me as she kept telling me before her wedding that she didn't want to go on her honeymoon. I didn't understand. Did she overhear a conversation about my dad having a procedure? We were very careful not to tell her then. Her soul knew something wasn't right. I convinced her this was her time to go and enjoy her new husband. She cried as though she knew something. She couldn't express it except she said, "I feel like if I leave something bad is going to happen."

Of course, I dismissed that energy and said it was because we still had fear about losing Mark, and this was her moment and nothing bad would happen. Until I had to make that dreadful call to my brother-in-law, and I heard her scream in the background. She said she felt so horrible all day, she kept seeing signs of the Divine Goddess. I told her he was in the hospital not doing well, so she could get on a plane and come home. Once she arrived home and saw all the cars, reality hit her. I will never forget her passing out in her husband's arms as she walked up the porch into the house. She passed out a lot that night. It was that night when I knew I had to detach in order to not go down with her.

The loss of my brother put all of us in a state of despair. This was when I began to realize how when you are grieving, you are very weak. I didn't have the strength to address things I felt happening around me. You see, during this time I suspected my husband was having an affair—a woman's intuition is always right; however, I choose to ignore what I felt. I wasn't ready for the next battle. It would take two more years for the next battle to begin, only this was not even close to a fair fight. I had nothing left. My cup was empty; I didn't even know how to fill it. I was grieving my dad, my marriage was ending, and my only concern now was my boys. Somewhere deep in the dermis was the grief for my brother that I would not open for many years.

As with any loss, if you allow yourself, there is a time to reflect and process the emotions that need to be released. I didn't get to do that for many years, however as children we do pick up, subconsciously, energy from our parents. Somewhere in the midst of my reflections of my dad, I remembered a vivid experience I want to share about his intuition. Remember we all have these gifts, whether we decide to use them or not.

My dad was a very religious man—he found peace by going to 7:00 a.m. Mass daily. He wore a scapular around his neck and spent more than two hours daily in prayer and meditation. I believe he tapped into higher states of consciousness. He had the gift of clairvoyance, seeing an entire experience before it happened.

One day when I was ten years old, the whole family was driving back to Long Island. My dad was driving, my mom next to him in the front seat, and all of us kids were in the back of our station wagon. We had been visiting my Aunt Mary's house (my mom's sister) for a Sunday gathering as we often did. We got off the Verrazzano-Narrows Bridge and onto the Belt Parkway, when out of nowhere, my dad yelled out, "Oh my God, the plane just crashed."

My mom looked over and yelled back, "Oh my God, John, the kids! What the hell is wrong with you? Watch the road!" All four of us kids were very quiet and shook up.

My mom continued yelling at him in Italian, "What is wrong with you? Where is your mind? Watch the road!"

My dad said, "I don't know what just happened, but I just saw my parents' plane crash."

Once again, my mom spoke rapidly in Italian to him. The translation is, "You idiot, your focus should be on the road driving our four children. You scared me and you frightened them."

My dad then said, "It's OK, kids. I'm OK."

My mom continued to talk to him the entire ride home.

Needless to say, I was worried about what he said. My

grandparents were going to be in a plane crash? Well, here is where it gets interesting. You see as we were passing JFK International Airport, my dad was actually doing something called "remote viewing"—with or without knowing it he was accessing his higher consciousness. That evening, once back in our Long Island home, I heard my parents speaking about what he saw. He was giving her such details, and looking back now it was an incredible moment in time. I also would understand my "high alert" as an empath at only ten years old.

A few weeks later, my dad went to the airport, as his parents, my grandparents, were flying back into JFK International Airport on an Alitalia flight. In those days, families would practically be on the tarmac waiting for arrivals. As the plane was coming in, my dad noticed it looked like it was landing too steep. He stood and watched as the plane's entire midline split in half! Can you imagine this is what he saw happening on our drive home a few weeks earlier?

Thank God no one was injured. My grandparents were in first class and the humorous part of this experience was my grandmother Ermenia would not leave the bags she had brought back from Italy. She had to go down a blown-up slide to disembark the plane, which she finally did, holding in both hands a bag of sausage and one bag of sopressa. My cousins were actually watching the six o'clock news and heard their Uncle John's voice as he was being interviewed. They were horrified and called my mom. It was a very upsetting evening until my dad walked through the door. It was very clear he had some kind of powers.

It was the front-page story in *The New York Times* on September 16, 1970, with the headline, "All 156 Survive as Jet Landing Here Splits."

Here is one of the newspaper photos from that day in 1970.

Photo: Bureau of Aircraft Accidents Archives

*****

As the years passed, I knew that he knew "things" that he didn't share, but his actions told me he knew something. One evening, I went to get some groceries, it was probably after 9:00 p.m. It was my very first time out since my second son Mark was born. I was taking my time, as other moms and dads know, as doing it alone was peaceful. About an hour later, I started my way to the checkout line. I looked up and saw my dad standing there! I was stunned and instinctively thought, *Oh no, what's the matter?* I said, "Daddy what's wrong?" Once you have experienced life traumas it makes you on edge.

His reply was, "Are you OK? Why are you out this late grocery shopping?" He definitely "felt" something. He loaded up my car, followed me home, brought everything in, and helped me put it all away. He didn't say a word to my husband. He looked pensive as he kissed me and went home.

The following day I spoke to my mom. This is what she told me. *Your father said, "I'm calling MaryAnna." My mom replied, "It's late, she's probably in bed." My dad said, "No, I have a feeling she's upset." He called my house, and my husband answered. When my dad heard I was out after just giving birth one week earlier, on a cold winter night in February, while my husband was comfy relaxing watching TV, he dashed out the door knowing I would be at the King Kullen store a few miles from my home.*

My dad actually got that intuitive feeling that something was wrong. Who knows—he never wanted to discuss it again. I believe he didn't share his true intuitive message that night. I know now that there was black ice everywhere. I was also very tired, not sleeping with a one-week-old baby and a three-year-old. Let's suffice to say he made sure I got home safe. The more disturbing part that my mom shared later was that my husband didn't care that I was out and wasn't even worried. He definitely was not emotionally attached to me or his children. Looking back, these were signs of narcissistic personality that would later become very clear to me.

Even clearer would be my dad's spiritual gifts, which will remain embedded with me. One week before my sister's wedding, my dad had a conversation with my husband

and me. Mostly to my husband, he said, "If anything should happen to me, I need you to promise me that you will do the right thing." He just kept repeating it over and over in front of me and my husband and my mom.

A very sick feeling came over me. What my dad was referring to were the many loans he gave us to assist in building our dream home. He not only knew on a soul level that he would be passing away in a few weeks, telling no one his own visions, he also saw what the destruction of my family would be. I realize that he saw many things regarding my husband, hence the grocery store evening. My antennae went up, my gut just felt punched, and my dad looked deeply into my eyes with such love for me.

At that moment, once again, I felt I was being prepared for something ahead of me, and it would be bad. My husband looked at my dad and made a promise he would never keep, nor did he ever have the intention. Later I would discover many things about what went on behind my back.

November 2, 1991 would be the end of many things. We all had to navigate without my dad, without my brother Mark—I felt like I was living a nightmare.

My life would never be the same. We had lived an upper middle-class lifestyle, and now my dream house we built together had to be sold and my soon-to-be ex-husband turned into someone I never knew. His actions were so self-centered—a narcissist, as I would come to realize later. He never once thought of our boys. It was all a chess game to him; he got pleasure out of my misery. He didn't pay child support for nearly ten years, and somehow, he got away with it. My kindness and love for my sons was greater than his darkness.

I waited ten years, until one day he slipped up by driving up to my home to pick up my son in a new expensive car. I was able to capture the plate and called the division of child support where I had a case number on file. He had the option to auction the car to pay his back support or keep the car and pay child support. He chose the latter, which took forever because he would pay just enough not to get a summons. The system is so broken—why did he get a choice?

I struggled to pay bills. I had three jobs, bought a small house, and did everything in my power to make it a home for my boys. It was always hard, especially because I wanted them to show respect and love to this man—I knew that was important. Deep inside it was always about them, my love was stronger in knowing it would be for their benefit. I didn't want them to hate a part of themselves, and I encouraged their relationship with their dad. I knew when they were old enough to understand and look back, they would be great men! I am human, and sometimes it was extremely painful. Unconditional love was something God had given me, one of my many gifts I would discover.

Affirmation

I am...

Root Chakra, also called *muladhara* in Sanskrit, is the first chakra or energy channel located at the base of the spine. The door to the core—Mother Earth. When in balance we feel connected to our physical self, safety, tribal and family karma, and courage. Origin of life force.

Vibration: C note "Lam" Earth

Color: red

Crystal: ruby can be used to balance this chakra.

Mantra

I am present moment awareness. I embrace life. I am grounded to Earth and connected to the crystalline grid. My body is healthy, my Earth body is a temple of my soul. I have the strength of source.

CHAPTER 2

Into the Dermis
(Sacral Chakra)

The guilt, the obsessed feeling of survival, dealing with the loss of my dad on top of the loss of my brother, and then my family, including my mom judging me because of my divorce, left me feeling so defeated. In the midst of this life challenge, I was working in a beautiful spa in Smithtown, New York. It was in a Victorian house that looked like something out of a soap opera. It reminded me of Pine Valley (for those of you who watched *All My Children*). The owner and I clicked the moment I met her. The entire team were hairdressers. I was the only aesthetician, along with nail technicians.

These women, especially Alisa the owner, became my support system. Many of them, fifteen or more years older than me, always had experiences to share, which were very comforting, especially Alisa and her husband Chris. I loved going to work—it was my escape. Until one day something happened.

During a facial treatment, I played the music I liked, which was mostly Enigma, or Gregorian chants, and this lightness came over me. There was a very peaceful feeling along with the movements of my hands like a dancer, flowing gracefully. It was as though I was receiving light energy. I now understand I was channeling light through me to my clients—a healing energy. My treatments were never the hour that was blocked off. I would try, but somehow ninety minutes seemed to be my treatment time. I would get so focused during the last part of the treatment massage it was as if I wasn't in my body. Clients also were telling me they were seeing colors. Let's just say it was more than a facial.

As I write this, it is twenty-one years after my dad's passing, and I got chills all over my body. I wouldn't realize for at least ten years what was happening to me. Each time I treated a client, I was actually going into a *moving meditation*. My clients were coming in for something more, and they were telling me they were experiencing an out-of-body feeling, and some mentioned experiencing colors. I felt amazing during their treatments. Hours passed quickly, hence the passion of doing something you love. It still would be another ten years before I truly realized what was really happening. Remember, my self-worth was still low, and while my soul was grateful and I felt blessed to be enjoying my work, deep down in my "dermis," I didn't really feel worthy.

That first spa I worked at taught me a lot. I moved on to another job full-time with a group of plastic surgeons. It was there that I realized I should open my own spa. I moonlighted with another laser company doing clinical training. A wonderful colleague encouraged me, and said I had these gifts, but I honestly was so embarrassed I couldn't receive even a simple compliment. I started to browse around at locations, but this wasn't something that happened instantly. In fact, I got a call during this time from the spa owner and dear friend Alisa. I will never forget that day—she told me she had ovarian cancer, was doing chemo, and was no longer running the spa.

I was devastated and I offered to come back and work and help on the weekends. Once again, I was numb, on autopilot. The scene at the spa felt so different—her spirit and energy were gone. The women I had considered friends and colleagues seemed different, just looking out for themselves. Without Alisa there I didn't have that same feeling and there was no *moving meditation* because I knew death was near, which I came to realize was another gift. I was invited to visit her at home, a place where we had wonderful parties over the years. I was scared because every ounce of my body knew it was bad.

She only wanted her family near her, but she also asked for me. My heart was heavy. I was overwhelmed to see her. She was fragile and had lost over forty pounds. She could barely talk; the pain was so great. I would go visit her a few times a week and each time I went I would bring her a small angel. It was my way of saying I am always here with you.

Within the next week, the call I had dreaded came. It was her son telling me to come right away. She had decided to stop eating and drinking and was ready to let go. I was honored to be there with her family, her husband, and one other dear friend to say goodbye. She was gone. My mentor, my friend. An enormous grief came over me. I said, *Oh no, oh no, I can't, I will not be able to continue.* So once again, I found a place to put my grief. I would not open that box for many years.

Instead of grieving, I felt I had Alisa's energy. I decided to turn the lower level of my small house into a spa. *Let me try it here first.* This way I would not have more overhead. I turned it into a sanctuary of bliss. I adorned it with angels. I had two large treatment rooms, and all I had to do was go downstairs from my house to work. I would be down there for ten to fourteen hours a day. It was there my moving meditation came back.

Life continued. I was treating clients and having the same healing experience myself. My passion was to help other women. I started a program called the Angel Wings Project. My blessings gave me the feeling of giving treatments to women who couldn't afford these "luxury" services. I reached out to a councilwoman at the time who assisted me in helping women with young children in shelters and providing them with treatments.

My mother was still with me then, and she was there the day we announced the program, which was picked up on local TV, right before Mother's Day. It was the most rewarding day of my life and also very emotional. I continued this program once a month giving services for free to women and listening to their hardships— it made mine seem like a cakewalk. I was grateful.

The spa was doing well, and I decided to sell the small house the boys and I lived in. I was expanding my business and opening an actual location in Roslyn, New York. My dream was coming to life. I was decorating and buying new equipment. I was busy with photo shoots, creating a website, and creating my own skincare line. The feeling of excitement was also taken over by fear of "What if this doesn't work?" It soon became a nightmare and a tremendous gift at the same time.

My sons were older—my firstborn had graduated college and my younger son was in his third year, about to embark on a year abroad in Florence, Italy. Life was good. I was busy at the new spa and loving it. My sanctuary of wellness, MaryAnna's MediSpa, was truly my sanctuary. Time flew by every day. I honestly had a hard time leaving this peaceful environment I had created, and I was very grateful.

On New Year's Eve 2005-2006, I hosted a big party at my house. It was a great night. I had moved to a large home after selling my small house. It was a rental, down the street from where I was previously. I felt I was able to give my boys back an environment close to where we had started, before their lives went through such turmoil. My younger son was leaving in a few weeks, and he would also be turning twenty-one. I took such joy, for the first time in years, having this New Year's Eve/twenty-first birthday party for him. I will always remember the sound of fifty or more twentysomethings singing "Happy Birthday" after the ball dropped.

That same evening, while I had many young people sleeping over, in the silence of the night I suddenly felt like my gut got punched. I felt such a deep sense of loss. Where was this coming from? A mother's worry he would be so far away? It reminded me of an awful, similar feeling when the same son was starting nursery school. He was crying, terrified of letting me go, or was he feeling my energy? Was it me who was terrified of my thoughts? The way I was crying was so much more. Something was trying to be released. Was it the grief for my brother? I just remember calling my husband, hysterically crying, and he basically hung up on me. I called my best friend Joann, whom I have been friends with since we were four—we grew up next door to each other—and she listened with love.

*****

The pain I was feeling was deeply embedded. I desperately tried not to let my son see my pain, but I couldn't shake the feeling. I knew he would be having an experience of a lifetime, traveling all over Europe. Two months after he left on his trip, my firstborn and I visited him. Once I saw him, the feeling was better, but it was like a poking pain—the kind you get when you have a bad headache, take an Advil, and the pressure is less, bearable but not gone.

I had such anxiety on the plane ride home. Why couldn't I just be still and figure it out? I just couldn't wait to get back to the spa and to my *moving meditation*. It would take me four more years to get the answer.

I did not find relief until eight months later, the day my son walked through the gate at JFK and I threw my arms around him. What I came to realize was his nursery school days would be the pain, or pay attention inward, that I wasn't ready to face. It came back with a vengeance in January 2006. My soul was trying to heal in 1989, but I pushed it down even deeper, deeper than the dermis, and made sure it was locked in a very secure box that I was convinced I never had to visit again. Boy, was I in for a big surprise. Then a few years later, I realized that my fear was also based on his age. You see, my brother was twenty-six years old when he passed, and it wasn't until my son Mark turned twenty-seven that on a subconscious level I found some relief.

In the winter of 2006, at my sanctuary, the first of many disturbing calls would stop my *moving mediation*. My aunt, who lived in California had passed away, which meant my favorite uncle Victor would be alone. I knew I couldn't make the trip at that time. My heart was heavy for him.

Then as we started the next holiday season, approaching 2007, I got the call that my godmother, my mother's only sister, my Aunt Mary, was in the hospital. She was six years older than my mom, a tough cookie, and she had lung issues. I spent a lot of time as a young girl with her and her husband, my godfather Uncle Alex. I loved being with them. They had three children, my first cousins, and we were all very close.

Unfortunately, those days were short lived, as my Uncle Alex passed away very young, when his youngest son, my cousin Frank, was only sixteen. Aunt Mary was a rock. I spent a good part of my summers with her as a teenager, too. It's interesting in healing our heart space...do we subconsciously take on the ways of our ancestors? Maybe I learned strength in just moving forward from Aunt Mary.

Once again, my heart was heavy as I realized through my own survival in life, I had missed the last ten years or more of my aunt's life. Of course, my mom filled me in, but I couldn't remember why I hadn't visited. I only remembered a time around the holidays when Aunt Mary and my cousins all came to my home in Smithtown, long after my dad had passed. Where did the time go? Aunt Mary's condition got worse. I was there with my mom, my sister, my uncles, my aunt, my cousins (her children) as we sat by her bedside waiting for her to let go after they removed life support. That was December 2007. My mom was devastated once again, another big loss.

Again, longing to get back to my *moving meditation*, the week started off disrupted. *Oh no, what is going on?* I was very distracted, with thoughts of worry, grief, and my mom. I began to panic because my *moving meditation* wasn't working. A panic attack was coming over me and I felt despair. Did I pick up everyone's grieving energy? Is life throwing me a new curve, another lesson? I didn't think I could take it. I *can't* became my new phrase, and another cycle would begin.

There is a time when you can really look back and understand the "why." What I have learned is the betrayal to your own soul for not giving it the love it deserves fills in a void that is a temporary fix. Some choose drugs or sex, but for me, my vice was fixing other people's problems. Hence, I began a relationship with a man with many problems. Now

I understand the reaction from friends and my mom, asking why I was taking on this. I couldn't articulate that this was a distraction from my own nightmare. My life wasn't supposed to go this way. Rather than digging skin deep, I chose to remain on the epidermis. Clearly, I had convinced myself it was a safer place.

I had pushed all the extreme pain into the dermis through the muscle, making sure it was alarmed now and secure. I was a champion at that. The irony of it was I was working on the epidermis of many people yet burying my own pain. Did I know I was doing this? I only knew I wasn't going to allow myself to be distracted enough that somehow I wouldn't get back to my sanctuary and my *moving meditation*. Dear God, is that so much to ask?

If only. If only I had known what was coming. My intuition wasn't guiding me now. My fire was extinguished from all the energy and healing I gave to others. I wasn't aware then of my energy field and the importance of my personal power. I didn't know that I was willingly giving it away. I was so drained, and the feeling became a new way of life for me.

Affirmation

I feel...

Sacral Chakra or second energy center is also called *swadhisthana* in Sanskrit. The sea of chi, the emotional self, sexuality, intimacy, vitality, passion, and creativity, relationships, emotional cording, control of life force energy, freedom.

Vibration: D note Vam water element

Color: orange

Crystal: carnelian can be used to balance this chakra

Mantra

I am God vitality. I am sacred sexuality. My emotions fuel my manifestations. I release lower desires of ego, elevate my emotions to a higher level. I feel the beauty of all creation. I deepen my love and connection with Mother Earth and Soul of Nature.

CHAPTER 3

Just Breathe
Solar Plexus

O ne evening on my drive home from a long day at the spa, my mom called and asked, "Where are you?"—never, "How are you?" Exhausted and cranky, I snapped at her and then began to tell her about my day. She listened and then said, "Call me once you are home." I could hear in her oice that something was wrong. I felt a wave of anxiety come over me—as if I was being punched in the stomach. *What now? Is there no peace for me ever?*

I called her as soon as I got home, and she told me that her brother sent a letter to the whole family and to check my mail. This would be the next wave of me once again knowing that death was coming. Her brother, my Uncle Tom, was suffering the past few years with similar issues like his sister, my Aunt Mary. And both he and my mother had open heart surgery fifteen years earlier, within three months of each other. My heart sank as I read the goodbye letter my uncle wrote to his entire family and his parish community.

He had been ordained June 18, 1949, as a Capuchin priest, to the order of the Capuchin Province of the Stigmata of St. Francis. The family said as a kid, my uncle had a calling, just like his older brother Victor. I remember thinking, *Wow, how cool God called them to this purpose.* His family, especially my mom, was so proud to say her brothers were priests.

Needless to say, our family car trip adventures were to lots of churches; it gave me a gentle feeling, the warmth of being in the back of the altar, the smell of incense. No one gets to go back there, and it felt special to be in this sacred area. My dad was always very serious, addressing his brother-in-law as Father Thomas, which seemed strange to me as a kid. As an adult, I came to see the great love and respect my dad had for him. There was a bond. My dad had gone to the seminary, which was more a time of confusion than a calling. I guess back then if you were raised a very religious Italian Catholic you went to the seminary, instead of therapy—kind of interesting, at least from my perspective now.

Uncle Tom had an amazing sense of humor. All his nieces and nephews, twelve of us in total, were baptized, took our first communions, made our confirmations, and were married by Uncle Tom. He even baptized my sons. We had our own priest whenever we needed one.

"It's the beginning of the end," I told my mom. I rearranged my schedule at the spa so I could take her to visit him immediately. Watching my mom and her brother was surreal. I was captivated listening to their childhood stories.

One by one, his friends came by, and I almost forgot he was very sick. It was emotional just being there for a few days. He was a gifted carpenter like St. Francis. He fully restored the beautiful Victorian mansion that was the retreat house for the parish. I remember him building a table for my mom to use for her new pasta machine, a sewing table for my sister, and countless other things for my cousins. He was always building something.

He was now fragile and very weak. I was trying to be strong for my mom. Finally, one day he said to me in Italian, "Come here... What are you afraid of?"

I answered, "Losing you."

I never was very close to him. He was very supportive and visited us quite often after my brother passed away, but I felt like if he was so close to God, why couldn't he help, which sounds crazy. Was I blaming my uncle for my brother's death? Or was I feeling jealous that he was my mom's older brother, a relationship that was snatched away from me. Clearly, I had unhealed resentment that I didn't realize at the time. When I would hear he was coming to visit, I would say I had other plans. I know now that he knew my pain. Seeing him would mean the box that was secured, locked, and alarmed would have a chance to be broken into. I wasn't ready.

Soon after he was moved to where he began his journey, in Beacon, New York. He had called my mom to say his chariot was awaiting him. We stayed with him as he was getting worse. This time, my mom was at his bedside, along with her younger brother, my Uncle Frank. His son, my cousin Tom, who was named after Father Tom, was also there. It was a long night. He was in a coma. My mom and Uncle Frank went to lie down, and my cousin Tom and I stayed a while longer. We both decided to shower (we were staying in this hospice for priests) down the hall. It was a very peaceful moment. He was just waiting for us to leave the room, and within ten minutes, he was gone—May 28, 2008. Another passing, a body put to rest, a soul lifted back home, a tremendous gift to be present.

Deep down in the dermis I had a sensation of pain. This was somewhat familiar, only it made me ill with fear—a fear that is very hard to explain. I just knew that my little fragile mother had begun her descent. I didn't know when because my body had to keep moving. I just knew that I would cherish every second, every moment. This time, I would need to let her know, somehow indirectly, that she was approaching the end of her journey as Marianna Pietrantonio Nardone.

I visited her every day. She lived with my sister and her family of four children, the youngest of whom were twins, and so full of life that it was a gift she had them, their daily activities, and their beautiful innocence. Along with my older niece and nephew, my mother was surrounded by them all. Sometimes it was a lot of chaos but the best kind. Every evening my brother-in-law would come home from work and sit with her—something they had done every day for twenty years. He had such love for my mom and a very close bond that was more like a son than a son-in-law. He made her laugh and they had their own relationship.

My mom made many trips to the hospital—ambulances were called countless times from May 2008 to February 2009. Her immune system was very compromised as she was battling pneumonia. The main diagnosis was congestive heart disease. One evening after work I stopped to see her. My sister was always busy with the twins and taking care of Mom like the Red Cross nurse, I would say, teasing her. I went into my mother's room, and she was in bed early that night. The moment I saw her I said, "Irm, she has to go to the hospital now!"

My mom begged me, "Please, Mar, if I go, I will never come back."

I had to insist, as I could sense her eyes looked weird. I had seen the look before when her lungs are full of fluid. It's like she was drowning...she could barely speak.

It would be the first Thanksgiving she wouldn't be with us, as she was in the hospital. My sister and I did all the usual cooking to be normal for the children. Then later we visited and brought her fresh food, including my specialty, pumpkin raviolis. Looking back, I realize my sister and I never really talked about it. We learned to go through the motions, taking care of everyone. I vividly remember making sure our eyes didn't make contact because we would then both lose it. I have a deep connection with my Aquarius sister. With such strength in her quiet demeanor, she was labeled "the quiet one." When she did give her opinion, it was a moment you paid attention to. Luckily for us, Mom came home after that hospital stay.

My sister and I had hope and faith that she would be OK—it was something we were taught. My sister would do her rosary many times a day, while I was on autopilot. I always brought my positive energy. One afternoon I arrived at my sister's house with extra energy. Mom was weak. We were all in the kitchen—the twins were coloring and we were having tea. I opened a kitchen cabinet to get cinnamon, and I saw a few papers in between the spices. My mom was telling me to leave it alone, the cabinet is a mess. My OCD kicked in and I began removing everything and organizing.

I took the few papers out and put them aside. Once the cabinet was organized, I felt good. As I mentioned earlier, subconsciously this always gave me the feeling of control. I then opened what looked like a recipe. It was in my dad's handwriting, and what came next, like other times as you already know from my story, was astounding. It was a beautiful note that my dad mailed to her in 1955. While they were dating, he had taken a trip to Italy with his parents. The letter said he loved her with his whole heart, and he couldn't wait to be back in her arms again. The last few lines were written in Latin, as he ended all his cards or letters with "Teodora."

"What is it? Please, Mar, read it to me," Mom asked. As I read it to her, she began to cry. "I guess this means he is coming for me."

I thought my heart was going to explode. Now the twins were crying, and my sister just looked at me, her eyes full of tears, too. I said, "Maybe my finding this was just a reminder of how much he loves you."

She responded, "I'm not ready. He can't come now... How can it be that all this time has passed? How can it be?"

She said the rest in Italian, *"Oh Madre Maria, ti supplico, per favore, aiutami Madre Maria."*

I hugged her from behind, and my sister distracted the twins. As I drove the mile back to my home, I asked my dad to surround her so she could feel his love. I also said, "Please wait...we're not ready...please, Daddy." But I thanked God as I recapitulated that moment in my head. I had been in that cabinet hundreds of times, and never had I ever seen that paper, or maybe I did, but like everything, there is divine timing. That was the day God used me to deliver that message.

What came next would bring me to my knees. I was having a quiet evening with my dear friend Tim, and we had just ordered sushi when my sister called.

"Mom was just taken by ambulance. I am in the ambulance with her." She told me to meet her in the emergency room. Tim immediately started crying. He had a close relationship with my mom, and he also knew me well. He drove me to Good Samaritan, only a few blocks away from my house. He stayed with me for hours, until I told him to go home. It took a while, but Mom was put in intensive care. It was more serious this time.

I never thought the day would come that my mom would pass. She was fragile and holding on. She went into the hospital in February 2009, and after watching her struggle for almost one month, I knew to prepare myself. Once again, I put on a superwoman cape, and I went to the hospital with positive energy every day. It actually looked like she was getting better. They say sometimes right before death, a burst of energy comes over you. I brought her a new flavor of gelato every night (I wasn't supposed to be feeding her anything) and she seemed to have taken one spoon and enjoyed it. I knew when she didn't want it, we were closer than I thought.

My sister and brother also went every day, and we took turns staying with Mom. By now she was in intensive care. I think we were all numb. My firstborn came to visit her after that day but I told him not to come. My niece, Giavanna, came one evening and my mom was in good spirits when she saw her, most probably to show her granddaughter that she was better.

The doctors told us her body was failing—she was bleeding internally. We had to make the decision as siblings to remove life support, that it is an act of love to release her. It is one of the hardest things to do. I could feel my insides trembling. I couldn't eat or sleep. I can't remember the exact date they removed the machines; her body would tell us. Then on March 12, I stayed with her all night. She looked up at one point and saw me. I said, "I'm here, Mom. I'm not leaving you." She was awake for a while, and then she seemed to go into a deep sleep.

Then about 3:00 a.m. I thought I saw something by the doorway. My mom was in a single room that was by the side of the intensive care station where they put the ones close to death. As I got up and looked down the hall, I saw a monk. I gasped, as I knew that robe was very familiar—was this my Uncle Tom's way of letting me know she was close? Wait a second, am I crazy? I asked the nurse if the monk could come and stop by to speak with me. Her answer was, "We don't have any monks visiting the hospital."

Clearly, once again being prepared, Uncle Tom came to me. Maybe, as always, I would receive a message to assist me. My brother came in the morning to relieve me. I went home and showered, and returned by 11:00 a.m. My sister was in the room with Mom and two very close friends of my mom's who were nuns, praying over her. All her tubes were removed, and her arms were "weeping," a term the nurse used as her body was releasing. However, the nurse said it could be hours. Something inside me told me to go over closer. The nurse said she can hear you talk to her if you want.

I told her it was OK, and she could go now and finally be at peace with her firstborn Mark and Daddy who were waiting there for her. I told her it was OK for her to go to them. I repeated it a few times; the last time was more like a whisper as I told her I loved her very much. My brother and sister were inconsolable. Within ten minutes after hearing my words she was at peace. March 13, 2009. Now my sister, brother, and I stayed with her for hours. My brother left first, while Irma and I remained until they took her to the morgue. We could barely stand. We got to the elevator, and when it opened, in front of us was my friend Tim. How did he know? He said, "I feel like your mom told me to come. It was the strongest feeling, and you also hadn't answered the phone for days, so I just came."

What a blessing it was for me and Irma not to feel so alone getting in that elevator. I will always be grateful for God putting him in my life as that part of my journey and the love we shared.

I had lost so many people with her, but this time she wouldn't be there to console me. The pain or loss of your mother is very different. It's a cord of attachment that feels like it's been severed. You feel like an orphan. I felt sick, so completely, truly lost. My sister, became distant. We couldn't help each other. This would be a new era, one without my mom—a chapter that I didn't know what to do with, and honestly, I really didn't care. I was drained beyond words.

In November 2009, I turned fifty. Yet another decade, a milestone! I thank God for the humor of my sons reminding me that I was half a century old. With my mother's passing I needed to dig deep, skin deep. I had to get into the dermis to begin my healing. I had no boxes left to secure. I was on shaky ground.

Affirmation

I will...

Solar Plexus or third energy center is also *manipura* in Sanskrit. Thy will is my will, personal will my will be done. Mental self, identity, ego strength, boundaries, practicality, destiny, world structures, possibilities.

Vibration: E note Ram fire element

Color: yellow

Crystal: citrine can be used to balance this chakra

Mantra

I align with my personal will and the will of my higher self. I surrender to my spirit. I am wise in my actions, balanced in my emotions, and peaceful in my mind. I am divine realization. I awaken my divine purpose and action in the world.

CHAPTER 4

The Light Workers
Heart Chakra

During the month my mother was in the hospital, I canceled my clients so I could be with her. My lease was up for renewal, and it was also in the midst of the mortgage/market crash. I would have to close my sanctuary of wellness in Roslyn—everything was going wrong. I didn't think I would ever find my *moving meditation* again. It was a very dark time and I have learned that in the darkest moments even more lessons or "tests" will come. I had become a low vibrational person, attracting the darkness—things or people that I had moved on from suddenly returned, one by one. My dear friend John said it as though they could smell the blood—energy vampires.

I have a pure and trusting heart and misread the intentions of these "friends," the energy vampires. I was weak and they took and took my energy. I was drained and could not understand why everything around me was chaotic. I had just lost my mom and I thought, *Is that why I am drained?* It was the wolves in sheep's clothing who took these dark moments in my life and took my light and my energy, which I didn't know I was giving away. For those that were fans of the HBO show *True Blood*, I felt like Sookie, the fairy who didn't know she was a light source, and the vampires fed on her. You would have to know the show to understand why I am referencing this. Was my power source completely gone and was it stolen from me?

What else can you take from me? I was grateful my younger son Mark lived with me. I knew it wouldn't last long because he was doing the New York City commute from Babylon. I cherished every moment with him. It was comforting. I knew intuitively that I had about one year alone with just him. Talk about not knowing where you are, who you are—that's how I felt the day he told me he was going to move into the city. I wasn't ready for the empty nest. But I only wanted to show him support—it was his time. I embraced it with a grateful heart.

It was time for me to get back to my spa, where I set up a small room in my home after closing my space in Roslyn. My energy was still drained. No matter how much sleep I got, I was depleted, without a compass to know how to help myself. What I have since learned is when your vibration is low, out come all the energy vampires in all shapes and all sizes. Past relationships? Oh, how they loved this depleted version of me. They see weakness and to them it's an opportunity to get back in. It's the smell of blood.

A past person was waiting to come to my mother's funeral, as if he was on a date with me. Bringing along his family members who, while I was grieving, were whispering in my ear, "He loves you. Give him another chance." I mean you can't make this shit up. The longer version of my story would be a fantastic movie!

When you're not healed you can't look at your own pain. That's when he stepped in, and I said no. After a few weeks of grieving, he was back at my door wanting to take me to dinner. I wasn't in my body. Mark was leaving to move into the city, and he invited me to move in with him. I was weak and I needed comfort. It was a false sense of security. I gave up my rented house, and stayed with him a few months, and then I moved in with my sister and her family.

I unpacked and settled in my mother's room. I felt so comforted at first, and then memories began flooding me day and night. Some were from my childhood, and I didn't have a box for that. I knew I needed to look for a job, maybe a doctor's office where I could bring my clients. And now all I wanted was space far away from my sister's house. I needed to get an apartment. My mother's depression was what I was feeling in her room—all her fears and anxiety. It felt like death to me.

I opened one of her drawers, and I couldn't believe it. There was my dad's wallet and keys and my brother's wallet. I believe she lived her life after their passing in a deep depression. She never went to therapy. She was just stuck. When I look back, I remember she was grateful for all of us. But she carried sadness inside a dark despair. I was feeling all of it—my head felt like it was exploding. I did, however, have the joy of my sister's twins who were young at the time. They made me smile from the inside out. I made them breakfast and took them to the bus stop. These were precious moments of grace for me.

I began looking for an apartment. I wanted to be far away, as though I would be removing myself from the pain. However, I was guided to a very special carriage house on the North Shore of Long Island, ironically close to one of my truest friends, Sandra, whom I had known for over fifteen years. Synchronicity is divinely guided whether we accept it or not. This carriage house was surrounded by trees, overwhelmingly covering the windows of this two-bedroom little gem. It would be such a place of comfort, grounding, and knowing I had my closest friends nearby. It was a blessing. I was even working within a doctor's office, also close by. I finally felt things were going in a new direction.

Other friends who knew I was living there were always asking me if I was afraid there. It was dark and you could barely see the carriage house in the woods, surrounded by trees. During the very first month of living there I was organizing something, which always gave me a sense of control and inspiration. I always tried to instill this concept with my children and nieces and nephews, that organizing an area for work, or beginning a new project, allows the flow of energy. This goes back to ancient feng shui teachings, that clutter of any form is a block. The chi or energy force that surrounds us creates who we are and needs to be cleared of clutter in order to bring more into our life experience. I strongly believe and follow placement and positioning that can either enhance areas of your living space or do the opposite.

The carriage house had a bedroom that you stepped up to get to. Memorial Day weekend, 2012, was approaching and I was organizing the bedroom and forgot the step down. The next thing I remembered was I couldn't breathe. I missed the step and took a fall like a cartoon—going up in the air, landing on my back, and hitting the bottom of the step. The wind was knocked out of me. In that very second, I recalled getting hit by a baseball to my chest, probably when I was ten years old, and I remember my dad putting his arm around my waist and walking me around the backyard, telling me to breathe.

So, I got up crying, and started walking back and forth in my apartment not knowing my dad was probably holding me up. I did that for at least an hour, until I felt I could breathe again. Then came the excruciating pain...now what? I decided heat would be good, so I got in my car, put on my heated seats, gained my composure, and drove around the neighborhood until the pain subsided.

Physical pain is the body's intelligence...it stands for *paying attention inward.* I knew, however, that once again, to deal with physical pain would mean I would have to stop and take a break—maybe even a week off. But I convinced myself that I didn't need to do that. It was Memorial Day weekend, and instead of following my body's intelligence, I ignored that this was possibly a time to heal and possibly open up a small box. Not a big one, for sure, because by now there were many boxes locked, alarmed, and sealed.

I knew I could begin with deciphering, or at least recognizing that sometimes the gift is the pain...meaning, falling was how I began to realize that I was going inward just a little bit or wait...*maybe not.* Instead, I distracted myself by going on a dating app! *That would make me happy.* This would begin another way of coping or fixing someone else, instead of going into the dermis—the epidermis would feel better.

Going on the dating app was a distraction. It was my ego talking and clearly taking over. It was like going inward and then something stopping me. I didn't recognize that my ego was in charge—clearly this was a sign that my vibration was low. Listening to your ego is like devil energy. Your ego, I would learn later, means *E G O Edging God Out.* Healing means to have compassion for oneself. When we are in the energy of ignoring our intuition or guidance, life becomes uncomfortable. We will attract, on autopilot, exactly the opposite of what our experience could be. We are all born with this inner guidance, and tapping into it is when you are in alignment with your higher self.

What did I attract on that dating app? I attracted a person who lived an hour or more away, unconsciously knowing that I didn't want to get too involved. My heart won't allow myself to be hurt—it is closed to any more pain. I attracted a younger man, who was emotionally unavailable, and who, I realized later, had special needs...meaning definitely on the spectrum.

This distracted me from my pain and my progress. Now I was stuck in a place of controlling the outcome, allowing myself to be exhausted by entertaining a weekend visitor. This relationship of sorts went on for almost two years. The lessons I learned after this period allowed me to observe my behavior from the perspective of the witness. Watching and recapitulating the events made it very clear to me that my self-worth was in need of repair. This experience further depleted my power, and it was during this period of time that I became aware of what my personal power actually was.

I began reading the book *The Seat of The Soul* and I had many aha moments with the realization that I was medicating myself with a dysfunctional relationship. It didn't seem that powerful at the time, however this was the point in my journey when I decided to move from the sanctuary of the carriage house. I was not only feeling guided, but I was also seeing guidance. There were orbs of light surrounding my space. Here is one of the photos I captured one evening while listening to my intuition.

There was a sense of urgency, as if I was being guided out of the woods for one reason—anytime there was a storm we lost power. We had already had a small hurricane and I was hearing that I needed to move to an area that was not so secluded. During these almost two years, inside me was a longing for my *moving meditation*. I was working on my clients in a plastic surgeon's office, as well as managing his desk three days per week. It was a craving to begin again.

I do believe there are no coincidences. While working at this office, I met a woman whom I recognized from being in the beauty industry. We connected on a high vibrational level, which is the only way I can describe the experience that would come next. She was definitely a spiritual person; she told me that certain "light workers," a new term to me, would be coming to her home, and she extended an invitation to me to join them on the weekend. She could sense my ego talking me out of going and she made sure to contact me a few days before to give me the time and make sure I was coming. She said that only a few would be chosen to attend, and I was one of them. Slightly concerned about what might happen, I pushed myself to go even though I had to drive an hour out east to get there. Her home was in a lovely beach community, in a very tranquil setting on the water.

Upon arriving, I felt very uncomfortable and nervous. I wasn't good back then at meeting new people or talking about myself or my feelings. There were six, mostly women, and of course my biggest fear was going around the room and introducing myself. I wanted to throw up, but somehow, I passed that part. Two women explained that they were part of Edward Cayce light workers or light energy healers. They explained their journey on this day was focused on teaching us about our auric fields, meridians, and blocked channels that can be opened through acupuncture.

The next part was about discerning what our blocks were, or our dominant energy. What came up for me mostly was the blockage of grief. Along with that discovery came a feeling of being judged among a group of strangers. However, after six or more hours we finished with a healing meditation. For most of that day I listened, and then appointments were made for the following day. I, of course, had no idea what they would entail.

I made my appointment, and it was expressed to me to be on time. I honestly didn't want to come back and although I agreed in my mind, on the drive home my ego convinced me this was nonsense—until the next morning when my friend who was hosting called me to see if I was on my way. I said I was going to be late and to please give my appointment to someone else, as I didn't want to hold up anyone else's time. She proceeded to tell me to just come, it didn't matter if I was late.

Damn, I thought I had gotten out of it. The guilt made me get dressed and go—spirit works in very mysterious ways. This time upon arriving all I could see was this huge oak tree on the front of her property. How did I miss that yesterday? I entered the house where the two "light workers" greeted me and immediately took me outside to the front of the house. We sat for about ten minutes as they asked me a few questions about my astrological sign. Then they proceeded to ask my permission for a healing session. At that exact moment, I realized there was a massage table set up under that huge oak tree. I wasn't nervous, and at that moment felt this would be good for me, assuming it was a Reiki treatment, which I was studying to finish my next level.

They walked me over to this massage table and then instructed me to lie on my stomach as they would be pulling out any traumas and working on my meridians. I just listened as they began. One light worker had her hand on my head, as the other was at my feet, and they instructed me to just allow my body to release. In less than what I believed was a minute, I began to sob uncontrollably. I was actually trying to stop sobbing, but it was something out of my control.

All of a sudden, the light worker who was at my feet came and put her hand on my back and within seconds she began to cough...I mean cough as if she was choking. I wasn't in my body. It felt like I was in a movie and then it came to me the movie was *The Green Mile*. I couldn't move my body, but she walked away while she was still coughing and the other light worker was soothing me and explaining that I was releasing trauma grief that was so tight in my body, it was embedded. The more I sobbed, the more intense the other light worker's cough and at this point the coughing turned into choking. It was severe enough that they had to stop and allow me to sit up and gave me some water. Slowly the light worker stopped coughing.

I honestly didn't completely understand until I drank the water that as she was choking and coughing, she had pulled out the energy of my brother the day he died. Remember, he was gasping and basically choking as both his lungs had collapsed. My body had taken the energy of my brother. I was more or less in a hypnotic state as one light worker began to ask me who had passed who had the lung issue. That day, part of my soul fragmented. I would not understand that meaning until a few years later.

I was holding on to it in my physical body. Was that part of the box, the big one, that was locked away under the muscle far beneath the dermis? How did they do that? I felt very light, as if I was floating. They gave me instructions about my energy, about grounding. They spoke of polarity and how mine were somehow opposite. Grounding would be vital for my healing. I believe they unleashed the beginning of me allowing my soul to heal, or at least uncover something that was trapped in my body's temple, not allowing it to go.

All I know is I left that day and stopped only a mile or so away at a beach, and for the first time in years, I allowed myself to feel my brother. I talked to him, I told him I missed him and loved him so much, and I was so sorry I couldn't save him. I had felt him so close in that healing session, yet I still felt this weight of guilt and I didn't know how to release it. Either way, on my drive back to the carriage house I knew that weekend was not a coincidence. I actually understood that my guides and angels were helping to heal me.

I would relive that experience in my mind over and over, grateful to the light workers and my friend who explained to me that I was chosen because I was a healer and needed to move into my purpose. In order to do that they were assisting me on my journey. Profoundly, after that weekend, I heard, *It's time to move out of seclusion.* I followed my guidance as if it were a GPS system as I went east of where I was living. I discovered an area I hadn't been in very often. However the weekend of my light worker healing, I did go home passing through this little town, Cold Spring Harbor, feeling an energy of joy and uplifting and saying, "How wonderful... Imagine having my spa here."

Affirmation

I love...

Heart Chakra or fourth energy center is *anahata* in Sanskrit. Seat of the soul, divine intelligence, intuition, love, multidimensional, avatar Buddha nature

Vibration: F note Yam air element

Color: green/pink quartz—high heart

Crystal: emerald, malachite can be used to balance this chakra—also rose quartz (high heart)

Mantra

My true nature is love. I forgive. I free myself from the past. I live in the present moment. I am new growth, new love. I open my heart to higher and higher levels of love. I am divine abundance. I am divine flow.

CHAPTER 5

Divine Beauty Potion
Throat Chakra

The next phase of my journey was apartment hunting near or in this town called Cold Spring Harbor—a divine experience. I began my search with a Realtor who said there was an apartment in Huntington, which is very close to Cold Spring Harbor. She said, "It's not very large, but I think we should see it anyway." I agreed. It was on a quiet dead-end street, with a detached garage that reminded me of my grandparents' home in New Jersey. My first thought as I walked up the front steps was that they were terrible—old, loose, and worn-out. But when she opened the door, an energy came over me.

The apartment was small but the window on my left looked out to the backyard and for some reason I felt a beautiful energy. I must have looked strange because the Realtor asked me if I was OK. I said, "Yes, I am better than OK, and I want this apartment." She now definitely thought I was weird because it needed work, including a full paint job, and

I honestly hadn't looked at much else to compare it to. However, I knew I was meant to be there. Remember, I was now listening to my guidance and, more importantly, to how my body felt.

She set up a meeting with the owner who said this had been his grandparents' home. They would be renovating the lower level so no one would be living there for a while. I signed a lease in September 2012, and was excited to move into this apartment—the energy felt wonderful. I had hired a painter and on my break from work, I popped over to see how it was going. I went up the stairs to find the painter was already finished for the day, but this was my first moment alone looking at the empty space. Once again, I was drawn to that window on my left with this beautiful feeling. It was much stronger than the first time. Something was telling me to go around the back and see what was under the window, so off I went. First, I stopped to throw away some garbage in the trash bin near the detached garage and while I was doing that, I felt magnetic pull—an energy that is very hard to describe except it felt like a rope was around my waist pulling me in that direction.

I did not resist this energy and I quickly walked over to the bushes and weeds. I looked up and noticed I was not directly under the upstairs window, but I was standing in the place that I could view from that window. I began to move the weeds and discovered something concrete in the grass. It was very heavy, but somehow it looked like a statue and that gave me the strength to lift it upright. I can barely describe the feeling that came over me when I lifted this beautiful statue signifying the Divine Feminine. I cried tears of joy. I don't know how long she was under those weeds, but by the time I had moved in, a half circle of daisies had grown around her, at a time of year when daisies don't usually grow. Here is a picture I took to remember that divine message of the energy of the Divine Feminine Goddess and how I could feel her light.

It was a moment of grace. Every morning upon awakening, I would open the window, weather permitting, sit on the roof and meditate while absorbing the energy of the Divine Goddess. It was a feeling of complete peace. I felt her loving energy evoke a place in my heart that was opening with ease. Once I allowed her energy in, miracles began to happen. I moved into the apartment right before the big hurricane, Sandy, and I remember how I listened to the inner guidance telling me to move to an area less secluded. I know now that the urgency I felt to move was so I would be settled before the hurricane. Although my new apartment was without power for two weeks, the carriage house area was without power for nearly one month.

*****

The first miracle occurred one morning while I was getting ready for work. I was running a little late and then couldn't find my keys. Now for sure I was going to be late, so I called my first client and explained I had to cancel her appointment. I was now very stressed about finding my keys. I was looking by my car to no avail and decided to walk around the back of the house and ask the Divine Goddess to help me locate my keys. I then walked back to my car and, to my amazement, found them right on the grass where I had looked before.

Something told me to go to the post office in Cold Spring Harbor and at that moment, I realized I now had time to stop in. I definitely was in a place listening to my guidance, so I drove to the post office, which is at the beginning of Main Street in Cold Spring Harbor. And then the second miracle occurred. Before I got out of my car I looked up from where I was parked and what do you think I saw? A sign in an upstairs window that said For Rent with a phone number. I called and found out from the owner that he had quite a few rentals in the area. He was nearby and agreed to meet me in an hour to show me some spaces. I was over the moon with excitement. Would I find my new spa location, and would I get back, after all this time, to my *moving meditation*? Was this really happening? It was a blissful floating feeling.

I explained what I did for a living, and he showed me a space that was the perfect fit for me. I signed the lease that day to begin MaryAnna's MediSpa in Cold Spring Harbor. My first beautiful location had been in Roslyn, but now this would be my location after losing my mom. It was a feeling of finding my way back, or my way forward, to begin again. This space was more than a sanctuary of wellness—it was a magical place that brought me back to life in so many ways. My commute was just a five-minute drive. The town basically closed by 6:00 p.m. and if I stayed at the spa till very late, it was peaceful. It was everything I wanted, and I realized I manifested it—I was very grateful.

Magical was my new normal. Every day the joy of being back in my own spa was a high, not only vibrationally but physically. I knew I was in my purpose, the feeling of love, the knowing I was protected. I was definitely experiencing my *moving meditation* everyday almost all day on every client. *Was I beginning to understand my power? Was I stepping into my power?* The word *power* holds strength just in saying it out loud. "He's so powerful," or "What a powerful moment," or "You hold the power."

Like Dorothy in *The Wizard of Oz* had the power all the time. Imagine the power we have when we come to the realization that we are constantly giving it away. I believe I was clicking my heels every day and suddenly feeling a sense of fine-tuning happening. It's like having a great signal on your phone. I will use my power wisely and when I feel my signal getting weak, I will recognize I need to recharge. What I was discovering was how to turn my power off and conserve my energy for when I needed it to power up. The lesson is in knowing the difference.

Magical moments happened in that spa. I will share two that I will never forget. Both were young women, embarking on marriage. They came in every two weeks to see me, as I had "bridal boot camp." I will suffice it to say that these beautiful women had already gone through very challenging life experiences. Both had first names that began with the letter *D*. I won't reveal their privacy, however I received channeled messages for both of them. It took my breath away as they were very specific, and it happened more than once.

I was their guide and it allowed them both, in different ways, to release (as my treatment room was a sanctuary to hold sacred space). It happened the moment they arrived—a feeling would begin within me. I can only explain that it was like a level of love would come through me; it would give me chills. And then, during their treatments, I would feel strong emotions that would bring tears to my eyes. A lightness would make me feel like I was floating. When the treatment was over, they would share something, and I would channel a verbal message back that would astound them, as only they would understand. Today, both of those beauties are happily married with beautiful cherubs of their own. The bond remains even though I no longer do my hands-on treatments.

I feel peaceful every day. I now stop myself from explaining when I feel overextended or my energy is weak. I am aware. My ego isn't happy these days, it seems lost, thank you, Jesus! Has my soul finally taken over? Have my soul and my human experience connected? It appears to be a resounding yes! Is this what my friend John Edward meant when he told me I just had to get out of my own way?

I pondered those words for years trying to figure what he meant, what message I was missing—it was another big opening, an aha moment. Then a memory of my son Vincent came over me. He was in the third grade, a very smart child. The school had called to say he needed his eyes checked. My husband and I took him that same day for an eye exam. Once we got the prescription filled, I remember driving when my son started saying, "Wow, Mom, look at the colors...look at those cars... Mom, do you see that?" I remember looking at my husband—I had no words and tears were streaming down my cheeks. My little boy really couldn't see. How would he know that he didn't see clearly until he got those glasses?

So, my message is: How do you know you are blocked until you are unblocked? How do you know you are depressed until the depression is lifted? I began to see my journey without judging myself so harshly. I was reading *Sacred Contracts* by Caroline Myss, and less than a year later, I found myself at her lecture in California, meeting her in person as she signed my book. Soul contracts are sacred— they are agreements we made with other souls to enable us to grow spiritually here on Earth. I think I started to really recognize the true Earth angels who I was so blessed to have on my journey. John and Sandra were part of my journey and gently guided me for many years as my journey unfolded. The significance and the gratitude I have for them goes very deep into the dermis.

*****

As I began my days with my heart full of gratitude, I found myself remembering a retreat I always wanted to attend. Years earlier, at my spa in Roslyn, I found myself very intrigued with the practice of Ayurveda. I had been a huge follower of Deepak Chopra for over twenty years, and in looking for more information about the study of Ayurveda, I came across Chopra education. They offered many different courses and retreats.

I was ready to expand my knowledge so that I could bring more to my clients in the way of holistic healing. Many of my clients would ask me what vitamins I was taking or what I was ingesting daily, as if I must have a magic potion. While I was flattered, I was very conscious not to give supplement advice, hence beginning my next journey. I signed up for a week course in California called Journey into Healing—the name alone says it all. However, I was so overwhelmed with signing up for this course and closing my spa for a whole week, that I barely read the entire program. But off I went, over the moon with joy.

San Diego is a magical place. The La Costa Spa, where Chopra education had their seminars, is gorgeous, and the day spa had Ayurveda treatments. I was pinching myself. This was a manifestation come true. I really made an effort to disconnect after the first meeting with the Chopra staff. It was a little overwhelming because I thought I was going to a retreat to relax. Instead, I got a very detailed schedule to follow on this week of "journey into healing." Each day I was to be at a 5:30 a.m. sunrise meditation that was outside on the beautiful, landscaped property with our group, followed by a yoga class, and then group breakfast. Now remember, I was embarking on something unknown at this gorgeous resort where I just wanted to rest. This was challenging my soul. I was thinking I paid a lot of money to be here so why was I trying not to participate in the entire experience?

It was strange. I felt strange because I had waited and wanted this for so long and now, I was sabotaging this experience before it began. Suddenly I realized it was just jet lag and I would recover. To my surprise I started getting phone calls from home...not family but lower vibration people trying to annoy me, including an old boyfriend from a very toxic family, confessing his love for me and wanting to connect right at that moment. OMG. I was asking myself, *Why is this happening? Why am I entertaining this conversation? Shut off your phone. You are in a magical place that is about you.*

I realized that I had posted to Facebook about what happens when you are done fixing other people. The call was in response to the post. This person was an energy vampire that I set myself free from, or did I? Why did I feel the need to answer the call? Something felt off. I wished I could be doing a treatment and going into my *moving meditation*. This was clearly a test for me. I could be distracted by this low dark energy vibration or I could immerse myself with these light beings, yoga, meditation, and Deepak Chopra! My soul was clearly ready for this journey into healing, even if my ego wasn't.

The first evening lecture began with Deepak and meditation. It was wonderful making new acquaintances and leaning on each other, expressing our anxiety and excitement. I found myself immersed and talking with people who had come from all over the world. As the days passed, I began to form relationships with a few special people. We sat at lunch together, saved seats in the auditorium for each other, and shared why we decided to embark on this journey. I began to feel a deep connection within myself. The days were purposeful and meant to invoke something deep.

This is why the first day or two I resisted the flow and tried to control it, which failed miserably. When I let the flow come to me naturally, it was the first time I allowed myself to feel vulnerable. I was giving a gift to my soul. I wanted to let go, but it wasn't until after a few different lectures that I realized I had a lot of fear to release. I also learned about giving and receiving love. I realized that I was only giving and not even open to receiving the love that was there in my life. Meaning I couldn't accept a simple gesture or compliment.

On or about day three, Deepak led the meditation invoking the soul questions. His voice was so soothing as he said, "Don't seek the answers...just ask the questions." Who am I? Why am I here? What is my dharma or purpose? Words that were my wands from that day forward. There were lectures teaching us how to meditate from very wise masters and guest speakers as we covered the connection of body, mind, and soul.

I will share one day in particular because this was my turning point. Even as I write about this day now, I can feel what my face felt like outside as the sun was so comforting. After morning classes, I was ready for an afternoon of listening to a great lecture from Deepak. I got so comfy in my space, and then Deepak explained we were going to do an important exercise outside—completely silent. I might add we were a group of nearly four hundred people. He and other teachers asked us to stand up, leave everything at our seat, and follow in a row of pairs as we began this long quiet walk.

We were all wondering what was happening. It made me nervous, and I was flooded with weird anxiety, like *will I have to reveal something*? Something was bubbling up and I couldn't push it away. We got outside and Tibetan chimes were ringing. One of the instructors explained that when the chimes rang, we would have one minute to face the person next to us, extend our hands, then hold hands, and just look into the other person's eyes. After one minute the chimes would ring again, and we would move to the right and take the hands of the next person, and so on.

I wanted to run as fast as I could. Somehow, I began to cry, and as I moved with this unknown group of people, one by one, others were also crying or smiling so brightly it was all in their eyes. One minute is a very long time to stare into a stranger's eyes. I didn't see color, I didn't see age, I didn't see gender, I saw love...just love. I saw pain, I saw sorrow, I saw regret. I wondered what they saw in my eyes...this was a very long experience.

When it was over, we remained silent and went back into the lecture hall. Deepak asked us to share our experience if we wanted to. He told us that this was a powerful exercise to show us that we are all connected. When looking into the eyes of a stranger, you are looking into a part of yourself, as we are all one from the same source. It was the most moving experience and that afternoon something inside me released. I felt light, I felt more connected to these strangers, and I had a feeling of complete peace.

The next few days I didn't even look at my phone. I was fully present and didn't want to miss a second. I was focused. At times I lost track of time—it wasn't important. What was important is that I was meditating, and I had managed to quiet my thoughts. I didn't want this week to end. I made sure I smelled the flowers and walked the grounds and absorbed every second of the beautiful essence of this healing week. Uncle Victor, who I was very close with, called to check in on me, but I was so immersed I forgot to call him.

There's so much to share I am finding it difficult to express. However, my experiences that week were the catalyst for my decision to take the teacher's path. Which would mean I wanted to learn to be an Ayurveda Life Coach with a program called The Perfect Health Lifestyle. It also meant I got to come back to this beautiful magical place four to five more times, in addition to webinars, books to read, studying, and taking tests, many of which would be online. It also involved setting aside weeks to return for treatments for our own healing, and at the end, a final exam, culminating in certification and a celebration as graduates. I knew it would be expensive, but all I wanted to do was learn everything I could, and a new version of myself emerged.

Affirmation
I speak...

Throat Chakra or fifth energy center is *vishuddha* in Sanskrit. The spoken word. Creative expression, gratitude, worthiness receiving, letting go, transformation through words, mantras.

Vibration: G note Ham ether element

Color: blue

Crystal: aquamarine, blue sapphire, turquoise can be used to balance this chakra

Mantra
I speak the truth of who I am with love, wisdom, and clarity. I am a divine expression. I express energy as language, the spoken word as an architect of reality. Spiritual attitude is gratitude. I am worthy to receive the blessings of life.

CHAPTER 6

No More Signs of Darkness
Third Eye Chakra

Many of us who began this new journey together were worried that once we returned home and back to our lifestyles, we would have difficulty staying with our rituals. I was concerned that the daily activities of this beautiful place would be hard to recreate, but knowing I had this new family of enlightened people was comforting. I had work in front of me and many books to read. Once again, life would unfold in a way that I could never make up. You see, as you rise in anything in life, your career, your success, anything that makes you grow will challenge others around you because human nature doesn't like change. Change is how we grow, how we expand and learn.

As you start this journey of ascension, lower vibrational people will try almost anything to create havoc. When you don't want to go back to that, you may lose these so-called friends. Dark energy may test you to see if, in fact, you have graduated to a level of ascension. I was figuring it out. What came next would be the biggest lesson and biggest betrayal to my soul.

In the first few weeks after returning to my spa, I was meditating and following the new rituals I had learned. Then I noticed I was not doing meditation first thing in the morning. I felt off and I began reading the first book that got me back into a groove, but I knew something was different about me. I was just trying to get used to this new information, but I also felt drained. I was back doing my *moving meditation* in joyful bliss, but at the end of the day I was completely distracted, and my energy was zapped. At the time, I didn't understand everything I now know about energy and my personal power, but what helped me was listening to Deepak's soul of healing affirmations. His voice and the messages brought me back to feeling aligned.

I also started to become aware of other energies. I was always very intuitive as a child, and this was a new sensitivity. When I would begin a treatment on my clients, I would instantly feel their energy, but I wasn't aware that I was absorbing their energy. Not good because that is why I was drained. Subconsciously, people are coming for comfort, and they can leave behind the negative part of whatever they have in their auric field. I, however, was absorbing their energy and feeling terrible, thinking it was mine. I thought I understood projection, energy fields, and energy vampires, but I was about to learn a big lesson. I would come to know a level of evil that I didn't expect.

We all watch movies and hear stories that are scary, but

somehow when you're involved in that energy, you don't see it coming. It's naive to think that evil doesn't exist. I always looked at people through the eyes of God. I know that sounds corny, but I would never see the darkest parts of a person; I chose to see only the good. We all have shadow sides, light and dark—it is part of our planet. How does someone become a murderer?

They weren't born that way. Life difficulties or abuse overtook their light...extreme abuse as children can cause very dysfunctional adults, some become very dangerous without getting help. Many of you can relate to the phrase *narcissistic personality disorder*. It comes in mild to moderate to severe cases, the worst being completely in a dark place like a Jeffrey Dahmer! A sociopath with no conscience can become a monster. It is a very real thing but not in my world then. I knew of a few mild cases of narcissistic people, and possibly moderate, but it was not in my reality then.

Here is where it is going to get very deep in the dermis (within my own self-awareness). The dark will always challenge the light. In fact, when the light is gaining strength that is when it is the *most dangerous*, because when you shine and are in the process of expansion, darkness wants you to fail, hence you will be tested. Remember I said we all have been born with the gift of our intuition, our GPS so to speak. It really does guide us when we are in alignment and listen to it.

I had learned at this time in my life that grounding myself was vital. I am a water sign for those who understand a rising or ascendant sign and moon sign. I am laughing as

I remember telling my dear friend John Edward that I was all water—rising Pisces, sun Scorpio, moon Cancer. "OMG, you're so fucked." Kind of funny now. Imagine what I came to understand that my watery natal nature clearly has no Earth, and it is hard for me to stay grounded.

What does that mean? It means that I am too much in my head, daydreaming. It means essentially, as I would begin to learn in Ayurveda holistic science, that I was a vata. Sensitive to energies, to cold temperatures, sometimes hard to focus...nervous energy. It also means I had to be on a schedule, and my routine should be clearly defined. It also means that when I am not grounded, I am susceptible to my auric field being tapped or used, as my energy could be easily taken.

As John once explained, when my energy is not grounded, I look like l am a butterfly on a very windy day holding on to a branch...barely holding on. Interestingly when I studied vata dosha, I learned it was associated with wind and air but not Earth. The description of the vata dosha was me exactly.

My point here is I was an easy target...just returning from a healing journey...still not fully understanding it all but very open and very vulnerable at that moment in time. Well, in came the tests...big tests like my gut was on fire, the kind of punch when there is danger or a feeling of going up a hill and coming down fast. That feeling was a big indicator that something was not right.

I was getting daily confirmations about a person whom I was dating. I ignored them. I somehow thought this would go away. I was single for a while, dating but not serious with anyone. I was distracted with this person...I wasn't on my routine...he would do things or arrange things that I didn't even question. Later I would understand I was being psychologically hit. A version of narcissist behavior I had never known and did not recognize the signs of, until it was too late.

Let's go back to my story about finding my new location in Cold Spring Harbor that became my sanctuary every day. I was blessed with clients and peaceful energy. I had everything I needed and was now learning to be a life coach on the Chopra global network. Could you now imagine that someone was able to convince me to close my business?

Just writing these words still alarms me. How did I give my power away? Why? I worked so hard to regain my *moving meditation*. I was foggy and didn't recognize my own energy. Friends and family asked me to stop and rethink what I was doing. This individual could win the Oscar for best performance in a leading role. He was so convincing that my family members were also starting to believe him. For many personal reasons, I will share only part of this experience to help other women understand that this is very possible. I am very lucky to be alive. It went to a very scary place, a place where I could have died. I am grateful for the people closest to me—my sons, who knew something was very wrong, and two of my closest friends, John and Sandra, who I knew I could trust with my life, were my saving grace.

Family and other so-called friends believed what this person was going around saying. He was trying to destroy my character. I would come to find out later after blood tests revealed that he was physically poisoning me. I now could understand the foggy behavior, the decision to close my business, and moving. I have heard it described as being *kidnapped* from your life.

I will not be able to give significant details, however this devil energy or darkness attracts other darkness. They work together with this energy. It can include black magic, psychic attacks, and illness—it is meant to cause harm. It is meant to stop pure energy from succeeding. Stealing your light is the worst kind of energy vampire. This is a sociopath without consequence. This is a human having an experience without having any light in his soul. This is the energy of Hitler. They try to take you down emotionally so others think you have lost your mind, or physically by either drugging you slowly, so you don't notice all at once when you become foggy.

You just follow along with anything. Financially they destroy whatever you have built, so in the end when all has been taken, they just move on to the next victim leaving a trail of lies and made-up circumstances. They also need to be the star of the show—at every moment this person's energy was destructive. The interesting thing is that they can't retain your energy once you are gone. This is what creates their cycle of seeking out the next victim. For those who know about this kind of relationship, when you begin to realize something is wrong, then the abuse gets worse, and in some cases is very dangerous to your physical body, because they have no consequence—except to win.

Moving on from this energy requires healing. It is one of the things I thought I would understand, however healing from traumas requires you to know exactly what happened. It took me months to regain my balance. Part of that time was to recapitulate the experience...fill in the gaps where I had lost time due to being drugged. The real story could be made into a TV movie of the week, but for the purpose of not giving this part of my journey unnecessary energy, let me suffice to say that it will be another book!

*****

In 2018, I decided to take my full healing and honor the traumas. A good therapist was necessary, as well as using my own gifts. I had taken the Perfect Health Lifestyle program with Deepak Chopra, and I began by going back through my journey from 2013-2015 and rereading my books. All the lessons seemed to be jumping off the pages and talking to me directly. As I began my process of being a student again, many aha moments occurred. I could never figure out once I became certified how I would teach this. Would I do in-person classes? Or an online course? Or maybe take sections of the course like the doshas, which help people to discern the true essence they were born with. But now I began to understand that in "redoing" the program I was certified to teach I would start my own healing that I would be able to share with others in my life coaching and the Ayurveda journey. It was crystal clear that I would use every single step I learned, use it all on myself, and share with the world in an online format or a book.

My process began with meditating every morning before I had coffee, then being grateful for the smallest things. Like calmness and quiet walks by the water. I was definitely still in fight-or-flight survival mode, and it was vital for me to ground and protect my energy more than once a day. I was challenged in the area of stability as my whole life of owning MaryAnna's MediSpa was now in the past. The most difficult part for me at first was not having patience with my-self—again another part of a lesson in healing I would learn.

In Ayurveda, body, mind, and soul are all connected as a multidimensional being. I was learning this way before anyone on YouTube was speaking about their healing or awakening experience. Everything is creation, including our physical body in the quantum field. Ayurveda taught me the importance of consciousness, that in order to create perfect health I would have to make changes in my awareness, thoughts, interpretations, and choices. I would learn and understand that the basic elements of nature are expressed in our individual constitution (doshas) enabling me to maximize balance and well-being.

I went back to the mantra given to me, reviewing each level of consciousness—the physical body, composed of three layers, the environment, a personal body, and an energetic body. The environment is our extended body. Each breath we inhale and exhale is a reminder of the continuous energy taking place between our physical body and our environment. Personal body is the majority of cells that come from the food we eat. Shankara, an ancient sage, named the physical body Annamaya kosha meaning the covering of food. We are what we eat.

I opened the Ayurveda workbook and read this statement, "Perfect health in body, mind, and soul requires that we pay attention to the food we consume to maximize nourishment and minimize toxicity. It also requires us to be mindful of what we ingest, in what TV shows we watch, anything on our phones or the internet we are also absorbing consciously or subconsciously." The energy body named by Shankara is "the sheath made of vital energy." This energy is known as prana. This is our life force and orchestrates cells into a vibrant living being.

The subtle body also has three parts—the mind, intellect, and the ego. The mind is the repository of sensory impressions. As we go through different levels of consciousness, our sensory experiences change.

Intellect is the aspect of what our mind discriminates against, makes decisions, and processes. The ego is the aspect of our being that identifies with the positions and possessions of our life, our self-image.

The field of pure potentiality is our personal domain, the collective domain, and the universal domain. Every individual has a personal soul with seeds of unique memories or desires. These seeds guide the course of your life to the fulfillment of your soul's highest purpose. The collective domain is the realm you tap into timeless history and live a mythical life. The gods and goddesses that reside within your soul have one desire, which is to express their creative power through you. Universal is the deepest aspect of your being—beyond space, time, and causality. This is the universal domain of spirit in which all distinctions merge into unity. It is known as *source* or in Sanskrit as Brahman.

As I mentioned, I would start my day with mindfulness meditation. Then I would go back and review my dosha or mind-body principle. The three mind-body principles are based on the five elements or codes of intelligence—space, air, fire, water, and Earth. All exist inside and outside of all of us. In the back of the book, you will find a list of all three doshas and a quiz to help you explore your dosha.

Let's get real for a moment in time. Was it easier to pour a glass of wine or two and eat a bag of chips? Hell to the yes. I am human. I had my moments during this journey. It also made me discover some other distractions. Some days when it felt hard to stay focused, another vice was going on Amazon doing endless shopping for things I didn't really need. This is all part of the process of discovering why you do what you do.

It's different for everyone, but one thing I know for sure is devil energy is always to distract you from your growth. Staying off social media wasn't easy for me either, yet another mind-blowing discovery of zapping your time. I mention all these things to bring awareness that healing from trauma is not easy. I interrupted here especially to make this point—discipline is necessary when you know that you must move forward. You, and only you, hold the power to change! Read that sentence again—you, and only you, hold the power to change—period.

My dosha is called vata, meaning the wind. If you recall, earlier I mentioned my friend John telling me I was like a butterfly on a windy day hanging on to a branch. In balance, a vata can be energetic, creative, adaptable, and a good communicator. Out of balance, and I definitely was way, way out of balance, I was restless, hyperactive, anxiety-ridden, worrying, inconsistent, suffered with insomnia, cold all the time, and I blamed myself for everything. My healing began when I started following the patterns of my behavior.

I needed a routine and to eat more grounding foods, foods with prana life force, not processed foods. I needed to meditate, get out in nature, and use the elements like primordial sounds of the ocean that were so soothing to me. I began keeping a daily journal, writing down ideas and new beliefs that were true.

I started my yoga practice that helped open my chakras and brought me peace. One day at a time, I began to raise my vibration. I spent my days creating new products for my website and ideas began to flow through me. I was staying on my daily routine, grateful to be alive. Healing my mind would be the first milestone to returning to myself, only a much better version. I was very blessed to have my sons whose love and support never wavered. I learned that creating, drawing, making soaps, and making new skincare products was so distracting for me. It would take hours, that felt like minutes to me. This was a time of using my energy in a very good way.

Doing anything you love, a hobby, a vocation that causes time to fly by, is my best advice for beginning any healing process. The mind needs to be distracted by a force to be reckoned with. Meditation is wonderful, but if you can't begin there, then maybe it's cooking or writing or organizing (one of my favs) this begins to move your energy in a new direction. I would journal, I would paint a wall in my house...oh my goodness the inspiration of doing that would invoke within me new ideas for my skincare line. I redeveloped my entire skincare line with healing Reiki energy while also recovering from many traumas. This was the time that I began to study crystals and paired the synergy of Mother Earth and crystals with my skincare products.

As my mind cleared and the fog began to lift, I would begin hearing that song, "All I Ask of You," by Andrew Lloyd Webber, from *Phantom of The Opera*. Some days very faintly because my soul was calling out to me, but somehow deep in my dermis was something embedded that resisted. I would go about my day and the more I meditated the more clarity would come as some visions of what I experienced started to emerge. I remember sharing them with John and Sandra, the only two people I felt I could trust who were able to listen with patience and validate what I was receiving.

From that day forward I would gain strength and understand that I was on my way back, patience was a gift I learned to give back to myself. I also began for the first time to understand the meaning of loving myself first. I had never done that, nor was I even conscious that I wasn't loving myself. I am by nature a giver and was always fixing others, which was my way of not addressing my own pain. Each day I would hear many songs in my head that were my soul and guides assisting me.

The one song "All I Ask of You," became louder and

louder. I remember walking on the beach one day in Westchester, one of my favorite places, and the verses were playing so loud in my head I finally began to cry and laugh out loud at the same time. The lyrics express a deep and passionate desire for love and protection and for someone to always be there, dispelling any fears or darkness. The promise of warmth, comfort, and freedom, providing shelter and light, and vowing to guard and guide, spoke to my heart and soul.

Affirmation

I see...

Third eye Chakra is the sixth energy center known also as sacred sight and *ajna* in Sanskrit: Intuition, clairvoyance, psychic abilities, divine memory, thought, imagination, vision sight, and outer hearing.

Vibration: A note Aum

Color: purple

Crystal: amethyst can be used to balance this chakra

Mantra

I awaken my divine memory, my memory of my multidimensional nature. I activate my inner seeing and inner hearing. I see clearly. I take actions that support my intuition. I trust my inner guidance. I understand synchronicity as divine timing. I am the master of my thoughts. I am an illuminated mind.

CHAPTER 7

New Beginnings
Crown Chakra

I got it. No more signs of darkness. I could hear my soul calling me. The only way to describe this moment in time is a divine moment of grace. My heart could feel this love so powerfully, I knew my vibration was high. I began seeing little reminders every day and my spirit guides would show me something that only I would recognize. As a child I could always hear things and know things. My intuition was coming back strongly. I listened to my guidance.

I was feeling it was time to move and I followed my guidance, which took me to Greenwich, Connecticut. I rented a duplex surrounded by trees. Clearly, like years before in the carriage house, the trees were very grounding to me, as is the water. I was consciously aware of what I needed to stay balanced, and I was ready to start a new blueprint, a foundation to be built on solid ground.

Greenwich was definitely where I was supposed to be.

I was destined to be there. I felt safe, not to mention it is beautiful, with many beaches and parks. Wonderful people would cross my path, all on high vibrational frequency. You attract what you feel toward you, good or bad. I knew instantly if someone was on a low vibration or had bad intentions. I also knew how to remove myself quickly. I am always going to be sensitive to energy and at this point, I have embraced it as one of my many gifts. It also meant I would learn to take protecting my energy to another level.

I was rested and once again guided to look for a job, this time in New York City. I just knew somehow that was where I was supposed to be. The commute from Greenwich was easy, and I got a job with a wonderful plastic surgeon. I knew the first time we spoke on the phone that it would be a good fit. I was guided there. The first six months were amazing. I loved everyone I worked with, and I loved guiding the patients through their surgical journey or transformations. I made some very deep connections and friendships in that office and had experiences with them I will never forget.

Then on March 19, 2020, we closed as the global pandemic hit. I will never forget getting on the train at Grand Central. There were only three people on the train. It was creepy, yet somehow comforting in a strange way. I will tell you I was never afraid, not for one second. I was able to be strong because my guides were telling me to, and I could feel that I was safe, and everything would be OK.

I know my sons were upset, and of course none of us had ever been through anything like this. There was a point when they expressed the unfairness that this was happening to them, as well as the feeling of anxiety and being trapped. I also had a dear friend who lived near me, who was close to my sons' ages. Nothing is a coincidence, and we would go to the nearby beach to walk when some restrictions were lifted. I helped her with her anxiety, and she helped me see how my sons were feeling, along with my nieces and nephews. I was grateful we had each other those few months.

During the month of May 2020, my firstborn son decided to go to Florida with his fiancée, as they needed a change of scenery to keep their sanity. He rented a huge house encouraging other family members to join them. They remained at this location for one month before returning to their NYC home. I visited them for a week as well, working remotely. It was so peaceful, and I was grateful to be with them. It was one block from the beach—my sanctuary. I got lots of messages from my guides while I was there. It was a time I won't forget, but I had to leave them to go back to work. It was June 1, 2020, and doctors' offices were reopening.

Nothing would ever be the same. As many of you know, the office had to go through all kinds of modifications. We also had to change our clothes upon entering work and put on clean scrubs. Our entire office procedures would change. Surgeries now required more testing twenty-four to forty-eight hours prior. There were more modifications for keeping everyone safe—no more waiting rooms and online consultations. It was stressful as we started this new way of working. Most of my family and friends were all working from home and were very worried about me in the city. I drove three days a week with my own sterilization process for my car.

It started to take a toll on me. I didn't notice it at first, but by the time September came, and my firstborn was getting married in a downsized wedding outside with masks, I could feel my energy depleted. And honestly my outlook was very different. Remember I now knew each day I had to love myself, although it was a work in progress. I also knew I had to decide what I wanted to do. It wasn't easy writing a resignation letter and leaving the office and the people I loved, including the doctor and his fiancée whom I had become very close to. With 2021 approaching, I knew it was time, and I had to find my way. I left at the end of December, and I will always have the fondest of memories of that office. What they didn't know was how much healing they had brought me. I was placed there divinely, exactly when I was supposed to be.

The global pandemic changed so many lives, so many people we lost. The essential workers put themselves at risk every day, the heroes who got us through. For many, it was also a time of great reflection, as it was meant to journey within us to evolve. There are still so many war stories of recovery. Compassion for the collective consciousness is necessary to not judge others' choices in getting vaccinated or not. I don't think people realize entirely that our thoughts project outwardly to the collective. The positive thoughts each of us have help raise the vibration of all. In the same way, adding negative thoughts or speaking negatively breeds more negativity. We all watched with horror as protests and racism reared their ugly heads. As we continue to encounter the world we live in, I continue to pray for peace, as life goes on.

In March of 2021, I made a decision to move to New York City, despite lots of opinions of friends and family, many of whom were leaving or had already departed to the country or suburbs. But my time in Greenwich was up. I knew it was coming like a gentle push. I wanted to find work again but without a commute. My close friend who lived in the city near where I was moving had announced she was also done and going to Miami. For me, though, I knew moving to New York City would be another chapter.

You see, during the global pandemic my younger son and his girlfriend decided to venture to South Carolina. I knew they needed to be outdoors. They had both lived in the city for years and they were beyond ready to go. I also knew the moment he told me of his plans that they were not coming back to New York. It was there they created magic, and a few months later they got engaged. It was very romantic on a boat with Frank Sinatra playing and dolphins jumping in the background. Soon after they bought a large beautiful house and started planning their wedding. Just like the time I had with him after my mom's passing, I knew he was exactly where he should be. That's the joy it has brought me knowing they have created a beautiful life in South Carolina. His happiness is my peace.

In May of 2021, I moved to the Upper East Side. I made my apartment my sanctuary of wellness just for me. I could find that peace now every day in my heart—no more signs of darkness. My younger son and his wife had a beautiful outdoor beach wedding in September 2021. Another blessing was that my firstborn and his wife were expecting their firstborn. I was in a blissful state. I found a new job that was perfect for me, working with doctors and spas as an account manager, bringing me to another level of helping practices grow and find their way after the pandemic.

As the months were approaching the birth of my grandchild, I was always connecting within each day—it has become my ritual. I wanted to make sure there wasn't anything in the shadows unhealed before my grandson arrived. He was born April 15, 2022, and I can only say everything I ever heard about double the love isn't really true. I don't have enough words to express what love this little cherub human has brought me. It was a gift of healing some things that were still stuck in my auric field.

As we are consciously aware, healing is an ongoing lifetime process of awareness and growth. Staying in the present is all we have. When old shit comes up, I address it and keep moving because I don't want to miss a thing.

Our family is growing. New traditions have been added. Each year we now look forward to spending Thanksgiving in South Carolina with the whole family. I have so much to be grateful for and I am blessed as each day forward reminds me how far I have come to get here. I have learned to take only the lessons and the pearls of wisdom. The most important part is I have fully and completely embraced every aspect of myself with love and light. I honor my journey instead of feeling like I made mistakes. That was an old story that needed to go. Making a new story is how we change the patterns and create new ones.

It requires taking back all my power, and yes, wearing my ruby slippers daily. It has become my daily routine, or I refer to it as my "daily addiction" a skincare serum I created and enhanced with my healing Reiki energy.

*****

Part of my journey was learning how in severe trauma your soul can fragment. What it actually means is part of your energy is lost, stolen, and exists separately from you. In other words when an experience appears life-threatening or with severe trauma, the soul may begin to leave the body as part of the traumatic reaction—in the same way medical shock is defined as a dangerous reduction in blood flow or loss of blood. Shock is a dangerous loss of your soul's energy. Every soul will experience it differently. For me, therapy helped in retrieving soul fragments. It took a few years.

How did I know that my entire soul essence was back? Memories that were lost all of a sudden returned to me. I fragmented many times in my journey, not just locking grief away. The experience, especially of retrieval, was difficult because it showed me the periods of trauma in detail that were very painful. Part of my healing was unlocking the boxes of grief but also allowing the memory or soul fragments back in. Some may call this shadow work. It wasn't the dark side of me, it was darkness done to me.

There was sexual abuse, something that required me to

leave a piece of my soul at an experience of severe trauma. I will add that it was not a family member. I was in the second grade and had to go into a reading resource room alone with a male teacher. In therapy, I relived that day, even the dress that I was wearing. It also was the same day that I had to attend an assembly with my mom in the evening. She didn't tell me what it was about. I was trembling, then I heard my name called as the first-place winner in the second-grade handwriting competition. She wanted me to be surprised. With inner-child work, many people talk about discovering later in life the sexual abuse they experienced as a child.

Earlier I used the expression, "kidnapped from your life." It happened to me in the second grade, and it happened to me in 2013-2014. That is why I was in a fog and gave up my sanctuary of bliss. My soul fragmented. Yet in another tremendous lesson, I discovered that because of my old subconscious belief that linked trauma to winning, or trauma to success, I unknowingly sabotaged my own success. Once again, how do you know you are sabotaging yourself until your awareness is open to receiving it? A huge block was removed once I received and accepted what I was subconsciously doing.

Affirmation

I know...

Crown Chakra or seventh energy center is *sahasrara* in Sanskrit. Doorway to the divine. Spiritual understanding, cosmic consciousness, knowingness, empty mind, inner peace, order, clarity, incarnational doorway, connection to source above.

Vibration: B note

Color: light lavender

Crystal: quartz can be used to balance this chakra

Mantra

I align with the divine. I am divine transmutation. I open myself to my soul, my higher self, through the sun, the galactic core, into the heart of the universe, the source of the great central sun is pure, invincible, and eternal.

Chapter 8

My Ruby Slippers

Inwardly is where all the answers are kept. It is the ability to be still, to be the observer of your own story, with non-judgment, to be the witness. Meditation is the awareness of your own thoughts, knowing that your journey here is meant for a purpose. Being aware of our collective consciousness that our thoughts and actions affect everyone. Everyone's journey will be different and unique. We choose our journeys and the people we are here with to assist one another and humanity. This is not a coincidence that we are here at this point in history. Consciousness is more understandable now—more people are awakening to their life purpose.

Release, release, release. Do this method of healing gently, easily ensuring that your identification with old patterns never returns. Work inwardly on fear, anger, and resentments. How do you start? You start with forgiveness. Forgiving someone releases you from the burden of carrying the energy of the experience.

Subconsciously and consciously, forgive yourself each day for anything that no longer serves you. Say it out loud. I clear myself from any roots and factors connected to this pattern of embedded cell memory.

I subconsciously and consciously release myself and forgive myself and repeat this daily. Release doubt, fear, anxiety—your ego is holding you with these emotions. Ask yourself daily the questions I was taught. Don't seek the answers, just ask the questions. *Who am I? What is my purpose?* Eliminate barriers. Stop internal criticism and stop gossiping about other people—be nonjudgmental.

In February 2023 I began another new chapter. A new version of myself has transformed. I moved my residence where I could be close to the water, and my balcony sits over the East River with breathtaking views. There will still be challenges. Difficult people will always test us. Hurt people, who haven't done the inner work, try to hurt others.

My rituals of meditation recently brought me back to remembering the story of my connection with the Divine Feminine Goddess. It is truly divine. One evening I was doing my bath ritual—I made apothecary bath salts with the intention of healing. The oil I chose, the herbs I add, are all with the intention of higher guidance of my soul. The labels came easy to me as I was inspired to call them Just Surrender. The bath salts are infused with clearing negativity frequency and are used to invoke healing, cutting emotional cords, and releasing trauma and attachments. Life force restored. Interestingly, I had begun the packaging when I realized I needed one for myself. Water flowing into the tub was a metaphor for allowing love to flow through me. As I put a beautiful jar just for me on the side of the tub, I started to hear some new songs, like something was being released because I was hearing—*When I find myself in times of trouble mother Mary comes to me*—the Beatles song.

Now each evening I looked forward to what I would receive. The songs got so intense—"Do You Believe in Magic?" I had to look them up on YouTube to listen to all the words and decipher the messages. The best one was, *I love you more today than yesterday. But not as much as tomorrow.* I was recently looking for something in my closet, and I found a book of Oracle Divine Goddess cards. My vibration was ascending to another level. What I would come to know is *I love you more today than yesterday*, was a message—a newfound freedom on another level.

For those of my close friends and family, I will pull tarot cards. Mostly I do them or use them as a tool solely for myself. I found these cards that I never opened, maybe because it was not the right time. I do, however, remember where and when I purchased them only two years ago. It is not a coincidence they were calling me as I was moving things in my closet in my new apartment. I began to shuffle the cards and I realized I have a statue of the Divine Feminine behind me (a special gift from Lourdes from a very special young woman). The feeling of a warm peaceful glow, like the time I found the statue, came over me. Remember I would climb out the window, sit on the roof, and meditate. The peaceful lightness of the Divine Goddess is how I started every day back in 2012. I realized that was well before I went to learn meditation with Deepak Chopra.

She reminded me of that feeling of peace, then the first card jumped out. These cards are beautifully designed and the first one said, "Our lady of soul birth." The message on the card read, "You and I have never been separated, though you may fear it to be so, my beloved one. Yet as you grow, I grow. As you suffer, I suffer. As you celebrate, I celebrate. When you rage and grieve, so, too, do I rage and grieve. Your journey upon this planet is held within my loving embrace and is my journey, too. I am with you always. We cannot be parted; I accept all parts of you and all parts of your journey. There is nothing to hide from me, for I am in your life with you. When you reject parts of yourself, you reject me. When you love yourself, you love me...Love me, dear one, love yourself, and your radiant soul grows into life, into light upon the Earth."

The message continued. Each day after meditation I would be inspired to pull a card, sometimes more than once a day. The messages were exactly in alignment to a question or my thoughts or deepest hidden desires. It is through wholeness that we can allow the divine presence to manifest through us. When we are open, we allow our soul to lead us into our divine purpose.

I get chills all over me, as she reminds me of the thorn and the bloom. Both of the rose, she is encouraging me to finish this book as the next card says, "It is necessary for my light to be made to manifest to surrender as my soul is birthing." Just Surrender is the name that came to me months earlier as I created the apothecary bath salts, and I have not even put them on the website yet.

Clearly the Divine Goddess has been by my side always—skin goddess was my tagline. There is an expression that whatever God or source has for you, no one can take away. My mission or purpose has become clearer than ever that the goddess energy, the Divine Feminine within me, is being guided to be an instrument of healing light, beyond the spa room, just as my products say. That was my intention that I wrote in 2018 when my son was redoing my website and logo.

I remember that day so clearly now. I used to have a Divine Goddess on my windowsill. She sat behind me, after returning from the beach one afternoon in the spring and I wrote my intention. I also wrote all the crystal cards that I would pair with their energy corresponding to the upper three chakras—the heart, the throat, and the third eye. These would be attached to the areas I was invoking. The cards came when you ordered a product, along with a mantra for meditation, and the crystal, even how to clear your crystal and charge with your energy and intention.

It was my son Mark who chose the colors, especially the green one he placed as the forefront of the products. He asked me if I liked it on the bigger products. I loved the green. He was the creator of all the colors that invoked me to decide which chakras I wanted to connect each product to. I am *sure now* that he didn't know he was channeling that. His creative energy would be the heart of all my products. Hence, I paired the malachite with the fourth energy chakra, which is the *heart chakra*. This stone is known for its transformative qualities. It enhances intuition and is very powerful for both physical and emotional healing of the heart. It also creates a strong energetic barrier from negative energies providing psychic protection.

The mantra is "I love." My true nature is love. I forgive. I free myself from the past. I am new growth and new love. I am in the present moment. I open my heart to higher and higher levels of love. I am divine abundance. I am divine. These words came through my higher self, the creative energy I was tapping into at the time. Completely aligned vibrationally—many creative people express this energy field of quantum physics. Like me at the time, it flowed through me. It is not something that just appears, rather it is a conscious or subconscious alignment during a creative experience. My son did that, during his alignment of creating my new logo and colors along with how they would appear on the bottles, and it is truly divine. My higher self was clearly ahead of my physical self or emotional self. It took time from all my life experiences and lessons to catch up.

Someone recently asked me what was one of my favorite movies. I instantly said *Avatar* puzzled by my own reply. But you see, that movie touched my soul. There is a part in the beginning when a Skyperson comes into the village of the Na'vi. The Na'vi people are fearful of this new energy, and at the same moment these beautiful light flowers begin to land all over the Skyperson (disguised as a Na'vi).

In that moment she knows that he is special as these floating flowers come from the sacred tree of souls. She teaches him about the flow of energy of the sacred forest, the energy that lives in everything—the souls of the animals are sacred, the plants, and every living thing. She takes him to the tree of voices, where they connect to hear their ancestor's guidance. To me it spoke to the essence of life. All life is sacred, the animals, plants, all living things—we are all connected. When we are in nature, the basic elements are expressed in our individual constitution. Deeper meaning was *I see you...*

Ayurveda derived from the Sanskrit words *ayur* meaning life and *veda* meaning wisdom. Ayurveda, the wisdom of life. From the Ayurveda perspective, human beings are not viewed as mere thinking physical machines but rather as fields of intelligence in dynamic exchange with energy and information of the environment. We are multidimensional. Once again, I was guided to this teaching years before the world would be ready to receive it. My higher self knew. I was definitely listening in 2013, first for my own healing, then as the planet would evolve, I would share it.

Finding My Ruby Slippers is my journey of giving my power away and knowing how to regain it. The magnitude of what my personal power is took many years and many lessons. It has brought me here, to this exact time and present moment to share my light, my journey, my lessons, and my love. I was told that when your journey has been tough, it is because your mission is a large one. Navigating it as a human experience was extremely challenging. Once I fully surrendered to my higher self, physically, emotionally, energetically, mentally, and spiritually, it has been better than the best ChatGPT intelligence that has me fully engaged—

there is no going back to that version in the past. This is the version of where my mission begins or my dharma was clear as day, like the song lyric, *I can see clearly now the rain is gone.*

I am a soul having a human mission guided by ascended masters and all the encounters with Earth angels and soul contracts I am grateful for. One hurdle after another, I surrendered. It is my intention, just as I mentioned at the beginning, that my story invokes a spark, a message within your soul for healing, raising your vibration for expanded consciousness, and guiding you to see your true beauty. Awareness of self-love creates a ripple effect with the collective consciousness when we love ourselves fully. It enhances every single soul, vibrating humanity to higher dimensions of love and light.

Once you have a new narrative, you have to make a new blueprint with a strong foundation that is built on your new narrative. Just as our phone requires a software upgrade, we must install our new software program for our soul, for this is the new version we have ascended to. Remember that the known is the prison of past conditioning. We have to continue to make new intentions each day and be present, for that is where the magic is. We are not defined by our experiences; our new software allows us to be an observer of our experience.

Today my ruby slippers don't slip off, not even for a second because my power is embedded in my soul with new software.

May your inner beauty be activated and your true soul essence glow.

Epilogue
Fountain of Youth

Nearly everyone wants to live longer, the desire to do so isn't new. Five centuries ago, the Spanish explorer Juan Ponce de León, searched for the fountain of youth. In the 1930s Americans became enthralled by the Hunza, a traditional people in the Himalayas, who reportedly lived past one hundred years of age. Now scientists are studying the centenarians of Okinawa.

While science is catching up, much of that science now focuses on nutrition—"You are what you eat." I heard that phrase when I was in grade school. Sounds so simple, right? Aging results from deterioration of gene function and cell metabolism. Nutrients form the foundation of our biochemistry; they can be used to fine-tune how the body functions at its most fundamental levels. We now know that inflammation is a huge part of how rapidly or slowly the body ages. Telomeres—specific proteins at the end of our linear chromosomes—can be measured to determine why some people age faster, where others seem to never age.

Our mind has the controls. Many of us are waking up and understanding that core beliefs we were taught are not true. Programming as an ancestral pattern is inherited, hence, we can alter our bodies in the most negative or the most positive ways. If your mind is holding on to a belief that fifty is old, because of an embedded thought or something you believe in, then *you will be old* at fifty. Again, "What we think we will become." ~ Buddha.

Nourishment For Body, Mind, and Soul

Long before there was a doctor who advocated eating fish for breakfast, I was repulsing my colleagues with my quarter cup of tuna with mustard and quarter pound of cucumber salad for breakfast. Self-taught, I learned more than twenty years ago that my twelve-ounce coffee with a scooped-out bagel would send my whole body into a complete trembling mess by 10:00 a.m. Can you imagine, I had a full day of working on clients, giving them my calming healing energy with a basic low blood sugar attack, and shaking, which are signs of possible diabetes. Blood work later would determine *no* hypoglycemia—it was food related.

It was a big shift for me. For the past five years or more, my adrenals and fight-or-flight mode were engaged in my life experience. I started by changing what I was ingesting, and then stopped smoking, a divorce-related habit I picked up, and last I had to learn how to balance my stress to authentically treat my clients with what I now realize is my gift of healing hands.

1997 was the beginning of my stress levels skyrocketing. I think it's a good place to begin my journey with anti-aging essentials. Back then, the *D* word (*divorce*) wasn't as common as it is today. It more or less was in my embedded subconscious that divorce meant you had failed miserably at your marriage, and along with that came lots of Italian guilt. I was raising two preteen sons, and all the single parents know exactly what comes with that. And we blame ourselves even when we know our spouse was the cheater.

In the midst of that life experience and being a single parent, I began a process of eating better...really *clean,* a term that wasn't known back then in relation to food! It was my body's intelligence that somehow I didn't resist. On another level, my soul knew, and just like that I began reading and learning about antioxidants and the power of nutrients neutralizing oxidation, aiding in free radicals. Let's just say I became obsessed with antiaging essentials. It took a few months to notice that I started to feel better, with more energy. My adrenals were shot, however, it would take years for me to come to that realization. As an aesthetician I saw firsthand how certain antioxidants have an amazing effect when applied topically, hence my exploration went deeper, bypassing the epidermis.

I didn't formally study nutrition, although all my clients wanted to hear all about it. I was careful not to tell them what to take. My journey was skincare, and I felt like I could be an example and inspire my clients with my combination of green juice cocktails and antioxidant vitamins, clean food and alkaline water, all related to the fountain of youth. Remember, "What we think, we become."

As I mentioned, I became obsessed with the power of antioxidants. What does that even mean? Basically, you want to neutralize free radicals, which are unstable atoms that can damage cells causing aging and illnesses. Free radicals, for example sugar, are known to cause inflammation. You can neutralize free radicals both inside and outside your body by boosting immune function through good nutrition, adding supplements, hormonal balance, detoxification, and purification.

I became a practitioner of Ayurveda, the process of consciously feeding your body's temple, and Body Intelligence (BIT), mindfully eating in a quiet environment, chewing for proper digestion, and extracting proper nourishment with foods that have prana or life force. That means no processed foods, eating the balance of the colors of the rainbow and following the dosha principle of eating foods that are aligned with your body's natural rhythm.

The most common cause of inflammation in our country is our high sugar diet. Too much sugar causes glycation, which is a spontaneous nonenzymatic reaction of free reducing sugars with free amino groups of proteins, DNA, and lipids that bond to chemically modify these proteins. AGE (advanced glycation end product) creates unnatural crosslinks with collagen protein and changes their shape, flexibility, elasticity, and function. The result is premature aging.

The two related reactions to impact the body's natural state of balance are inflammation and glycation. They manifest themselves as aging throughout the body's organ system, most apparently in the skin. The major antioxidants you should get plenty of are as follows:

• Vitamin C, found in plants and fruits.

- Vitamin E, specifically high potency tocotrienols. (There are two forms of vitamin E, tocotrienols and tocopherols).
- Coenzyme Q10, found naturally in our cells, decreases after age twenty (basis of the 1978 Nobel Prize in chemistry awarded to Peter Mitchell, PhD who found this vitamin is needed to make energy in every cell of the human body.
- Alpha-lipoic acid found in plant and animal sources.
- DMAE dimethylaminoethanol found in fish.
- Carotenoids phytonutrients found in red, yellow, and orange flesh of plant leaves, flowers, and fruit.
- Flavonoids are found in green tea, isoflavones, red wine, and resveratrol.
- Resveratrol is one of my favorites, and can be found in purple grape skins, blueberries, and cranberries. You can also supplement, as I do, with 1000mg. Resveratrol is associated with greater longevity, extending your telomeres.

As with anything, balance is the key...eating along with your body's natural rhythm, just like following the natural circadian rhythm in nature, is the key to vital health. Nourishment is needed for the body, as well as the mind.

Research has shown how important our gut health is to our mental health. Did you know that 70 percent of your brain health is linked to your gut? This truly encompasses the "you are what you eat" statement that has been around since I was a kid. Digestion takes on much more, including everything we watch, read, or say. How does our body digest emotions? Or watching a violent movie on TV?

"Know that all healing is from the arousing of the divine within each cell of the body."

~*Edgar Cayce*

*****

Next to breathing, eating is our most vital bodily function. Energy and information are converted into our body's intelligence. Food must be nourishing, our digestive system must be strong, and evacuation efficient. In Ayurveda, our digestive power is called *agni*, or internal fire. When we have a strong fire in our digestion, we will extract the greatest level of nourishment. When our digestive system is sluggish and evacuation is slow this may lead to toxicity, undigested food, constipation, fatigue, low energy, and brain fog—in Ayurveda this is called *ama*. We want to create more agni or fire, less ama for optimal digestion, which in turn creates the balance of your body's health. Here are some suggestions that I used when embarking on my Ayurveda teacher's path.

- Don't eat unless you are hungry...especially don't force breakfast if you are not hungry.
- Don't eat when you are upset.
- Always sit down to eat.
- Reduce ice-cold foods and beverages.
- Listen to your body's appetite—digest one meal before eating the next.
- Stop eating when you are satisfied, rather than fin-

ishing your plate because you feel bad about leaving food.

- Don't engage in eating while driving or watching TV—these distractions will most likely make you overeat.
- Eat in a quiet environment, bringing awareness to your chewing... actually enjoying the taste of your food. I actually found myself full much sooner when I chewed well and wasn't distracted.
- Be aware of being conscious or present in that moment.
- Relax after a meal by taking a short walk.

*****

In the appendix you will be able to take the dosha quiz, which will help you obtain your dosha and the foods to enhance or to balance. I was very surprised when I learned that all the salads and green juice were not helping my body's constitution or dosha. I need more warming foods, like soups, sweet potatoes, and oatmeal. I am a vata/pitta, much more vata as you will read about later.

I have always had digestion issues, which I never understood until I learned that my digestion was very weak. I learned how to stimulate my digestive fire with fresh ginger fifteen minutes before eating. I also added digestive enzymes to assist me. Eating all the great organic food didn't matter because my body's digestion wasn't absorbing any of it.

Ayurveda taught me to include all six tastes at every meal. We will accumulate toxicity in our mind and body whenever our life experiences are not completely metabolized. Both physical and emotional digestive systems must function in order to extract optimal nourishment. Conscious awareness helps us to identify where we are storing toxicity in our physiology. Gentle cleansing can eliminate accumulated impurities in the body and mind. Harmonizing our internal rhythms with nature is the key.

The ebb and flow of the tides of nature perpetually exchange energy and information. Each cell, tissue, and system in our body expresses a rhythm. When we are in balance with nature's rhythms, we will experience more joy and vitality. Getting outside into nature is the process of understanding that every cell in our body carries the same intelligence as nature. Almost all plants and animals are entrained with nature's rhythmic cycles.

- Circadian rhythms. The twenty-four-hour cycle of night and day created by Earth spinning on its axis.
- Seasonal rhythms. The twelve-month cycle caused by the rotation of the Earth around the sun.
- Lunar rhythms. The monthly cycle of the moon revolving around the Earth.
- Tidal rhythms. The gravitational influence of the moon on the waters of the Earth.

The cycles of nature influence our mental, emotional, and physical well-being. I was the woman who stayed up very late, "a night owl." Then I was so exhausted and sluggish in the morning, drinking coffee in excess to keep going. It took me some time to change that routine. Once I found myself waking up without an alarm, doing my morning meditation, and, weather permitting, going outside, everything began to change for me. I also was tired early and found myself very easily beginning a nighttime ritual to wind down and go to sleep early. Most of my adult life I was up very late...I told myself it was a peaceful time for me, a story that I wanted to believe. It was a pattern of behavior that I was doing on autopilot. Now, the most peaceful time is 5:30 a.m., some days, even earlier. In the appendix you will find my daily skincare rituals and my "cocktails."

Appendix

- MaryAnna's Skincare Rituals
- Skin Goddess Beauty Cocktails Recipes
  for Glowing Skin
- Testimonials for MaryAnna Skincare Products
- Ayurveda: The Science of Life
- Dosha Quiz

MaryAnna's
Skincare Rituals

Cleansing, cleansing, cleansing. If I had a dollar for each time I have explained how to cleanse, I would be a billionaire by now. Here is what every woman needs to know. First, absolutely no hot water or facing the shower and letting your face be hit with hot water!

I am always amazed at the stunned faces looking back at me with that "WTF are you saying?" expression. Hot water dries out your skin, so if you love to feel squeaky clean, you are actually throwing your skin's pH into overdrive. In essence, if you remove too much oil, your body will produce more oil to catch up. Dry sensitive skin will be dryer and you can get blotchy, patchy-feeling skin. Overmoisturizing will also not compensate. You will feel dryer and your skin will drink it up and require more. Once again, balance is the key. Instead of washing your face in the shower, I teach how to cleanse properly with cotton pads and recommend using bottled water for those who suffer with skin impurities.

Most women, especially younger women, are product

whores, trying all the latest bells and whistles and sparkly new trends in skincare and skincare tools.

Exfoliating

There are many misconceptions about skincare, like exfoliating or using harsh scrubs or rotary brushing, which are not new by many means, ladies, just reinvented. I believe I got a Bonne Bell battery-operated handheld brush under the Christmas tree in 1975, as my mom already knew I was obsessed with my skin. Skincare companies instruct overcleansing and scrubbing your skin, like it's the kitchen floor—*stop the insanity.* Just because you see a beautiful model on TikTok doing it doesn't mean it is OK. It's wrong, wrong, wrong.

Exfoliating is important, however, it can be accomplished by topically applying a retinol product that doesn't need a prescription. There are many very good over-the-counter retinoids that work. If you are using a retinol product, then you most definitely do not want to scrub. Prescriptions, like Retin-A that your dermatologist can prescribe, can help the epidermis to slough off dead skin, as well as over-the-counter ones.

Skin has cycles that are twenty-eight to thirty days to fifty to sixty days depending on lifestyle, medications, and abuse of alcohol and of products that are too harsh. Let me also add that you aren't able to clean those brushes properly once wet bacteria gets in, so you are reintroducing bacteria onto your skin daily.

Scrubbing or using any of these rotary brushes, which

claim to remove dead skin, also tear capillaries, causing broken blood vessels and patchy blotchy red skin. My advice to clients over the years has been to get harsh exfoliating out of your system, spare your precious face, and scrub your body as much as possible. Treat your face as if it is a satin pillowcase and each and every touch can cause a wrinkle. I know it sounds extreme—I watch how roughly women apply even simple creams. My point is to be gentle, gentle, gentle, and if you practice what I preach you will see results fast. My clients have seen a huge difference just stopping the shower cleansing. Using a gua sha stone is also great as long as you are gentle, and it is a wonderful way to do light lymphatic massage.

SPF

I cannot emphasize this enough. Use at least a SPF 20 every day, all year. In the summer and warmer climates closer to the equator, you should use a SPF 35-50 daily. Anything over 50 SPF is full of chemicals. In case you didn't know, the FDA has never approved anything over SPF 50.

Tanning beds still exist, but I honestly don't know why. In just fifteen to twenty minutes, the amount of UVA (aging) and UVB (burning) is magnified as though you were at the beach for four to five hours. To me, it's an insane choice to expose yourself to rapid skin damage or possibly skin cancer. Today we have so many other great options for spray tanning, even ones that come from plants like beets, with no nasty chemical smells. Gone are the days of looking orange. Today's spray tanning or at-home tanning kits are natural-looking. I have my own personal favorites like Love My Tan made by an Australian company. You can find it on Amazon.

Daily Skincare Routine

The morning cleanse should be a splash of tepid water, unless you have gone to sleep with makeup on, a big no-no, or did some other fun activity that requires you to cleanse again. A simple basic is first layering a humectant, like my Daily Addiction, mostly hyaluronic acid, which restores a thousand times its weight in water. My formula is made with plant botanicals and flower essences, as well as being infused with my Reiki healing energy. Follow that with a light moisturizer if you need to, then SPF, unless your makeup has SPF already in it. Be mindful that SPF is the last thing that goes on your skin.

Unlike hair care, where it is recommended to switch shampoos every other month or so, skincare loves consistency. So, let's get your gorgeous faces ready.

Always cleanse your skin in the evening. This should be done with tepid water on cotton pads, applying cleanser in upward motions until the last cotton pad is clean. Now your face is ready to apply one of the treatments of your choice. This is the time to do a hydrating mask once or twice a week. Evening is always about treating the skin, using a moisturizer or night serum, eye gel or cream, and neck cream. Remember all products go a long way. Don't overuse. It will only end up on your pillowcase.

Add a humidifier to your home or sleeping area. And

remember, no scrubbing, no hot water, no facing the shower with hot water, and no rotary brushes that are too harsh, in addition to spreading bacteria due to no sterilization. And FYI, hot water or alcohol doesn't sterilize rotary brushes.

If you suffer with very dry skin or live in colder climates, take omega-3 fish oils to lubricate from the inside out, add a teaspoon of coconut oil to a shake or drizzle over a salad. One teaspoon daily will dramatically aid dry itchy flaky winter skin.

I know that in the past five years everyone has become overly obsessed with skincare, but please leave the chemical peels and microneedling to a professional aesthetician. I have seen more horrors of permanent damage from at-home treatments. Just because you can buy it, please know that you can cause injury that is irrevocable.

*****

Self-Love is Not Selfish

One of the biggest lessons I have learned over the course of my life is to be patient and fully and completely embrace and love myself. I have been practicing this lesson for a while, and it's interesting how I now speak to myself. Instead of looking at "flaws," I tell myself how beautiful I look, or how great my body feels. Our words are our wands. Self-love is loving yourself unconditionally, even on days when you feel you didn't do your best. It's acceptance and allowing your divine self to shine through.

Do Something Just for You

What has helped me was truly putting myself first. My morning rituals, my meditation, and making my healthy shake are all ways of loving myself. I make sure I have the healthy foods I require on hand, including all my other rituals for nighttime bathing, my essential oils for my salt bath, and taking my hot yoga classes which, I know, are very good for my soul. I make certain to do these things just for me. When I don't make the time, I feel the difference. Ask yourself, "What have I done for myself lately?"

Remember, self-love is not selfish. When your cup is full and overflowing then you are giving to others from the purest place of love. You will not resent giving time or your energy when your needs are fulfilled. Young mammas I think have the idea, however we can get caught up in all the things we need to do in a given day. Be mindful that alone time in the bath can be such a wonderful respite in the evening—make it a ritual, light candles just for you. Listen to soothing music. You will be surprised how much happier you will feel by doing something special just for you. The house police aren't coming to check that you left dishes in the sink.

Go outside and take a walk alone. Just listen to the sounds outside and find your own thoughts. Find something that you love to do. It can be the simplest smallest thing like watering the flowers in a garden. Make it your special time to reconnect and go within. Try not to use your free time to browse Instagram or TikTok—that's an energy drain. Use your alone time off and away from electromagnetic fields.

Meditation and Healing Music

When friends or clients ask me how to begin meditating, I usually send them guided meditations from YouTube that are five to ten minutes long. The healing frequency music is also one of my favorites to have on in the background when I'm home, as I always want to encourage myself to be on a high vibration. I pass this on, as healing through sound is a powerful modality. Music heals the soul. Primordial sounds are the vibrations of nature, the wind, a rainstorm, birds singing, and the sound of waves crashing, these are all primordial sounds.

Mantras are used to quiet the mind, the repetition of repeating over and over in your own mind, which gently distracts you. Of course, the mind goes elsewhere. This practice takes time to get to a place of stillness. Mostly I encourage people to start just simply with your breath and closing your eyes. Some find it helpful to stare at a candle or sacred geometry. Our chakras, or energy centers of our body, have unique sounds that help to enliven or balance. Crystals also are powerful tools placed correctly in or around your chakras while listening to the tone or vibration of each energy center. As a Reiki master, I use crystals all the time while performing a treatment to rebalance the chakras.

Did you know that through touch, the skin releases a pharmacy of chemicals that have health-promoting effects on the physiology? In addition to feeling good and relieving tension, your own loving touch can detoxify the body's tissues, calm, and enhance your own immune system. In Ayurveda, the self-care loving massage is called *abhyanga*.

I do it every morning with lotion. In Ayurveda it is done with oil. Oil for me is best in the evening. There are certain oils that will help pacify or stimulate your dosha. Calming oils are best for the evening and stimulating oils or lotions for morning.

Skin Goddess Beauty Cocktails Recipes for Glowing Skin

Cucumber Refresher

- 2 medium-size cucumbers
- 32 ounces of filtered water—alkaline water is best.

Wash the outside of the cucumber well, leave the skin on and slice into large circles. Be mindful not to slice too thin, as you will be placing the cucumbers in water and too thin will make it dissolve.

Fill your favorite pitcher with water, place cucumbers in, and refrigerate or leave out. You can add slices of lemon or lime, as well.

Within 15 minutes the water will start to absorb the flavor of the cucumbers—drink it up. You can continue to refill the pitcher for the entire day using the same cucumbers.

Cucumbers act as a natural diuretic and anti-inflammatory. It helps us gals with bloat, midmonth, or anytime or when we overindulge too much sodium or alcohol beverages.

Also, you can take a few extra cucumbers and cut them into half-moons, place in a Ziploc bag, and store in your freezer. Apply under and on top of your eyelids for a quick anti-puff treatment before a night out. Or try in the morning for a quick fix for swollen eyes. Leave on for ten minutes, splash with cool water, and follow with your morning routine. It's a refreshing way to give yourself some love first thing in the morning.

Goddess Elixir Tonic

- Small or medium-size seedless watermelon, melon, mango, or papaya all are 9.0 alkaline. A body that is more alkaline is a body that is less likely to get sick—a known fact.
- One small lime
- Fresh mint leaves (optional)
- Six ice cubes (use your alkaline water to make ice cubes)

Cut the watermelon in half, scoop out all the watermelon, and place in a blender (or whatever option you chose), all the juice of one lime, and six ice cubes and blend!

Pour into a cocktail glass. The mixture will be slushy. You can add more ice if you want it more liquidy or less for a more slushy texture. Add the fresh mint as a garnish.

Watermelon, melon, mango, and papayas are all naturally sweet...be mindful that after 6:00 p.m. this beauty water has natural sugar. It is very healthy, but it is best to consume this earlier in the day.

Chopra Center Ginger Elixir

This elixir was designed to jump-start your digestive fire... one ounce before lunch and dinner approximately fifteen minutes prior to eating.

- 1 3-to-4 inch piece of unpeeled fresh ginger root
- 4-6 lemons
- 1 cup purified water
- 3/4 cup raw honey
- 1/4 tsp black pepper

Cut the ginger into small pieces. Using a powerful juicer, push the ginger through the juicer and juice enough to make one cup.

In a citrus juicer, juice the lemons to make one cup of lemon juice.

Combine the juices in a large bowl.

With a wire whisk mix the water, honey, and black pepper into the ginger and lemon juice. Whisk until blended.

Store in a pitcher or glass jar in the refrigerator. Don't chug the whole thing...just one ounce is recommended. And word to the wise, it has a *kick*!

Testimonials for MaryAnna Skincare Products

"Skin magic."

~ *psychic medium John Edward*

"Magic in a bottle, plant-based stabilizing pH tonic gives you that extra cleansing and removes excess oil while restoring your skin's pH balance. I can't get enough of literally watching those pores shrink. Leaves my skin plump and glowy. I am addicted...must have!!"

~ *@barplay*

"You need nothing more than this skincare line created by MaryAnna Nardone. Creates a beautiful slate for our amazing makeup team. Daily Addiction, Hydra Overdose, my skin thanks you."

~ *Alicia Coppola*

"I have raved about her skincare products. I use them—love the moisturizer, the Daily Addiction serum, the refresher spray. The new Bentley Just for Men collection. The actors that sit in my makeup chair have also commented positively after using on them—beautiful skin equals less makeup and always looks better in HD."

~ *Chris Burgoyne*

Ayurveda: The Science of Life

Emotional freedom is the foundation and one of the healing parameters in the Ayurveda Perfect Health Lifestyle.

Ayurveda: The Three Mind-Body Principles

Vata dosha: The Wind Principle
Primary function is movement.
Qualities of vata: Cold, light, dry, irregular, rough, mobile, quick, changeable. An individual whose mind-body constitution shows a preponderance of the vata principle will likely possess attributes that resemble the wind.
Physical characteristics: Thin light frame, variable digestion, dry skin and hair, cold hands and feet, sleeps lightly, lacks sexual stamina, moves and talks quickly, restless or hyperactive.
Temperament: Welcomes new experiences, resists routine, is a lively conversationalist, and spends money easily.
When in balance: Energetic, creative, adaptable, shows initiative, good communicator.

When out of balance: Tends toward mental agitation, anxiety, worry, inconsistency, insomnia, delicate digestion, constipation.

Stress response: What did I do wrong?

Pitta dosha: The Fire Principle

Primary function: Transformation

Qualities of pitta: Hot, light, intense, penetrating, pungent, sharp, acidic. Those with a predominance of the pitta principle have a fiery nature that manifests in both body and mind.

Physical characteristics: Medium build, strong digestion, thinning or gray hair, warm body temperature, perspires easily, sleeps soundly for short periods of time, strong sex drive.

Temperament: Sharp intellect, discriminating, direct, precise, stays close to routine, courageous, good teacher/speaker, spends money on items that enhance prestige.

When in balance: Bright, warm, good decision maker, strong digestion.

When out of balance: Angry, irritable, excessively critical or harsh, judgmental, aggressive, intimidating, skin rashes, burning sensations, indigestion.

Stress Response: What did you do wrong?

Kapha dosha: The Earth Principle

Primary function: Protection

Qualities of kapha: Cold, heavy, solid, stable, smooth, slow.

Those with an abundance of the kapha principle are typically grounded and steady, remaining unruffled by and sometimes resistant to change.

Physical characteristics: Heavyset, smooth skin, thick hair, sweet face, deep sound sleep, slow-moving, regular digestion, gains weight easily, and has difficulty losing it, good stamina, slow and easy sex drive, process-oriented.

Temperament: Easygoing, patient, thoughtful, stable, content, devoted, loving, comfortable with routine, saves money.

When in balance: Steady, consistent, loyal, strong, supportive.

When out of balance: Dull, inert, needy, attached, congested, overweight, overly protective.

Stress Response: "I don't want to deal with it!"

Visit maryannanardone.com to take the dosha quiz.

Acknowledgments

This book is woven with love and gratitude for the many souls on my journey.

John Edward and Sandra Coehlo, my gratitude is deep in the dermis as I hope you realize the impact, unconditional love, and support you have had in my life. As we get older it's even more important to keep the circle small. I consider myself truly blessed to call you family...soul brother and soul sister. Thank you for being on my journey as we continue and allowing me to be on yours. Precious memories with Justin and Olivia to be continued. Love you all.

Marianna and John Nardone, my precious parents, thank you for playing your roles excellently. Love you both deeply until we meet again.

My siblings Mark, IrmaRose, and Andrew, for being on my journey with me and for all the love, memories, and grief. Our bond will never be forgotten. IrmaRose, I am very grateful to have you as my sister. I love you very much.

My daughters-in law, Catherina and Fallon, for your love and unconditional support. I am so grateful to have you both...you are more like my daughters every day.

Uncle Victor, Aunt Mary, Uncle Tom, Uncle Frank...precious moments in time on my journey

Barbara Jacobs Pozen, my witchy special friend, who for ten years encouraged me to write, write, write. Thank you for all the love and support beyond your expertise during a crucial time in my experience and all the protection, aka book two.

All my clients over a span of five decades. It has been an honor to have been a part of your journey and serve you... thank you for allowing me to use my gifts.

Diana, my soul sister. Well, you just know I love you to the moon and back. Thank you for all the love and for allowing me to be part of your journey as we continue.

Desiree Fumento Gazza. For bridal boot camp, thank you for always shining your light, my Desi, love you.

Joann Bisconti Imbo, special thank you for over fifty years of friendship, our childhood memories, high school, and then our children. Your loss was deeply felt. I miss you...I will never forget how you held me up after Mark passed. My love for you and your family will never end, another soul sister.

Giavanna, Anthony, Bianca, Joe, and Alex, you have all brought me different levels of love. Thank you for choosing me as your auntie. I love you all very much.

Alicia Coppola, thank you for introducing me and my products to The Studios at Paramount. We instantly clicked in 2016, and your friendship over the years has meant so much to me.

Patricia Smith, what can I say? Sixty years of friendship and family...even when time passes, we reconnect as though it was yesterday. Your love and support when we lost Joann, I will never forget. Love you, Patti.

Tim Cilen, thank you for coming into my life exactly when I needed you. It was a roller coaster ride, lots of fun memories. I will never forget your love and support when my mom was dying. Love you.

Deepak Chopra and the Chopra community. Thank you for creating a time and space that was sacred for me to join on my healing journey. Taking the leap on the teacher's path for Ayurveda was divinely guided. I want to thank the entire dedicated Chopra Center team for all the love and support. Especially Tami, who still guides me by answering all my DMs. I am truly grateful.

Dr. Rap and Ashley, thank you for all the love and support and the time I spent working with you both will always be a special and sacred time to me.

Elisa Gorman, thank you for allowing me to be part of your ending...my heart knew you were close. I know you are exactly where you should be.

Cheryl Benton, for your patience and attention to every detail of this publishing process. I am very grateful to have had you on this first book journey with me.

Lorenzo John, thank you for choosing me to be your Nonnina. My love for you is beyond words. I am grateful for you every day. You have opened my heart to levels of love I didn't know were possible. My little prince.

About the Author

MaryAnna Nardone is a truly unique beauty professional. Her career spans over thirty years in the field of aes-
thetics. She has traveled the globe as a clinical trainer for
laser companies and has created her own holistic skincare
line, using the power of crystals and chakra energy fields.
She owned her own boutique, MediSpa, in New York City
and Long Island, and traveled to clients on the West Coast.
Her passion and purpose are guiding women and men on
their transformation journeys, in the field of skincare and
plastic surgery, as well as the Ayurveda holistic lifestyle.

She is an educator for Deepak Chopra's Perfect Lifestyle Program. She has celebrity clients in Los Angeles and New York City, specializing in her unique skincare and Ayurveda treatments that embody a deep knowledge of the skin. Her use of Reiki incorporated in her treatments is a powerful healing experience. Her passion and purpose in her everyday encounters with patients and clients are where she thrives. She uses her intuitive energy, wisdom, knowledge, and her own life experience to guide her clients with a combination of body/mind/spirit, wisdom authenticity, and trust.

MaryAnna created her own charity program called Angel Wings in 2004. She was featured in an article about women in business by Joe Hefferon for *The New York Times* (June 18, 2012.) She was called a light worker, and truly a "diamond." He wrote, "Sometimes you find spectacular in the midst...maybe that is where it works best...the wings of angels beat silently."

www.ingramcontent.com/pod-product-compliance
Lightning Source LLC
Chambersburg PA
CBHW070716130626
46553CB00005B/2019